Reality & Probability

Joseph Kahuho Gatoto

Reality and Probability

All Rights Reserved

Copyright © Joseph Kahuho Gatoto

All rights reserved. No part of this book may be reproduced or transmitted in any form or any means, electronic or mechanical, including photocopying and recording, or by any information storage and retrieval system, without permission writing from the publisher and or author.

Author Details

Joseph Kahuho Gatoto has been serving as a young adults and teens Pastor at Calvary Worship Center since 2012. He is a trained Journalist (Shang Tao Media Arts College), Certified Coach (CDI – Africa), Certified Public Speaker (ACPS), Poet, and a graduate from African International University (NEGST) with a heart to teach the integrated gospel, and integrate men to eternity in order for them to live an integrated life.

Kahuho38@gmail.com

Phone: +254715656938

Facebook: Kahuho Gatoto

Facebook Page: Integrated Reads – ILM

YouTube: Kahuho Gatoto

<u>Books in the Reality Series</u>

1. The Pneumatic Nature of Reality
2. Metaverse: The Metaphysical Nature of Life
3. Reverberation
4. Energy
5. Presences (TBA)
6. Reality and Probability

Available globally on amazon.com

CONTENTS

ACKNOWLEDGEMENTS

Special thanks to Agnes Macharia for helping me choose the cover design for this book.

Glory to God for the gift of writing and for the revelations from His word and in His word.

DEDICATION

To they that have understood to believe and have come to
understand that we believe to understand and they that seek
to believe to understand.

INTRODUCTION

Realities are contained in mind and are actualized from mind through a process that entails several processes that engage the faculties of the soul and the microcosmic realities of the soul that are in and themselves generated by the working of the soul and the becoming process of the soul from the womb. It is to these that I delve into in book 5 of the reality series with an aim of invoking the reader to consider their own soul reality and bring them to a place of intentional living.

There are pages dedicated to understanding the realities that are in the soul, probable realities, that are in mind, from which we decide what possibility to actualize.

Chapter 1

POSSIBLE REALITIES IN ETERNITY PAST

"In the beginning, God created the heavens and the earth."

Genesis 1:1 NKJV

The earth that is, and was, begun in the beginning, this beginning being in God and a moment in Eternity past in God, was a possibility amongst eternal possibilities in the person of God in eternity past. It is so because an eternal being has infinite possibilities which are unfathomable to the finite man. These infinite possibilities were in the mind of God, who alone can fathom them, and were as a result of His understanding. It is because we understand that possibilities are. Without understanding, there are no possibilities, and as such, these possibilities were birthed from the mind of God and in the mind of God having proceeded from His understanding. It is from these possibilities that God decided which versions, as it were in Him, to actualize in eternity past, which is a moment in God who is the Moment of His moments. Now, we must understand that this includes the spiritual realm and its inhabitants, angels. But we must understand that in His possible realities; of the physical realm and the beings in the physical realm, the prevailing thought in Him was beings that can understand as He

1

understands (beings in His image and likeness) which can, by that virtue, reverberate Him and be in fellowship with Him and therein delight in Him; for without understanding there is no delight in anything. We understand and therefore, delight. Understanding precedes delight. It is understanding that is the bedrock of free will. It is because we understand that we can will, and it is because we will to understand from understanding that we can decide to understand. And so it was, that God actualized the possibility of willing beings from possibilities of beings which would not will and from various innumerable possibilities of thinking beings as to how they would be in form and how their world would be in form. They were, then in Him, who is the perfect being and whose understanding is as such perfect. Which means that God knew the infinite possible realities from knowing the perfect possible reality of the realms which He had willed to create having understood their being in Himself. It is, therefore, by virtue of His perfectness, that God knows all possibilities inherent in Him willing that which is the perfect possibility; that is to say, God can only will that which is perfect from Himself, via His understanding, and in His understanding being from His understanding and therein by His understanding, which is perfect as He is, for beings are their understanding and the understanding of God is perfect, and in willing the perfect, He knows all else that is not perfect. His knowledge of the perfect, being the Perfect One, does not mean that He does not know the imperfect, rather by virtue His knowledge of the perfect, being perfect, and the Perfect, He knows all the imperfect possibilities, which in this respect are the endless possibilities of how the earth and the spiritual realm and the beings therein could have been like. By that aforementioned virtue, all these imperfect possibilities existed in His understanding as the perfect possibility existed in His understanding; for when God conceived creation, the idea of it, He conceived all its possible realities in Himself being all-knowing. Omniscience is such that the knowledge of a thing, such as His knowledge of creation in Himself, leads to knowledge of all things relating to the thing, creation, in and with all of its possible realities from itself and in itself and as it relates to it. God, therefore, knows all possible realities from our reality as it relates to one man and all men. They are before Him now, as they were then in eternity past. God knows all that can be and will be from what is and from what He wills and these, He has known from the beginning that is Himself in eternity past beyond Genesis 1:1. By the aforementioned, we find that it is because beings, of which God is the Supreme, understand that there are possibilities. Understanding precedes possibility. An infinite being, God, has infinite possibilities, whereas a finite being has finite possibilities. God can, however, only actualize the best possible reality in Himself, through Himself, by Himself, and from Himself; for He is a perfect being and all that He does is perfect as His understanding is perfect and the Understand of understanding- the Mind of mind. And inherent in the best and perfect possible reality actualized by God are infinite best and perfect possible realities to be actualized by God, through God, from God, and in God Who actualizes, by virtue of His perfection- and being that which is perfect- and therefore the Perfect One, only that which is the best and perfect possible reality. The understanding of God, from which the infinite best and perfect possible realities reside, is infinite and unsearchable. God, Who is His understanding, is unsearchable. It would, by virtue of the aforementioned, take infinity to actualize by Infinity, from Infinity, through Infinity, and in Infinity these infinite best and perfect possible realities, which would necessitate as an indisputable prerequisite, that man be infinitely united to the Infinite through, by, from, and in the Infinite One from Whom and in Whom, the finite becomes infinite as opposed to Infinite, for He is Infinite, the Infinite One, He is Infinity and to be united to Him would necessitate infinity from Infinity, that is a proceed of endlessness from Him that is endless and the Endless One that is without a beginning.

Chapter 2

THE POSSIBILITIES IN EDEN

"...let us make man in our own image and in our own likeness." Genesis 1:26-27NKJV

God is a thinking being and creating man in His image and likeness meant to create another thinking being, that is one with an understanding and, therefore, one that is able to understand and as such one that is able to actualize possibilities in his realm by virtue of possessing and having understanding. For as previously established: understanding precedes possibility. Man (generic) was created to exist in a realm with possibilities having become from varied innumerable possibilities in God of how and what he could have been like. Same as to Eve, the woman, who was created out of the man for the man. Both the man and the woman were created to become and are becoming beings, and it is through their becoming process that they birth particular possibilities inherent in which are possibilities; for every actualized possibility generates possibilities which are invisible in the sense that they are not actually in existence but are actual in mind. Actual in mind because every actualized possibility exists in mind prior to existing from the mind through understanding and in understanding through understanding and from understanding. That image and likeness then, that men (generic) were to reverberate was in understanding from which and in which, being through which and from which possibilities generate and are actualized. It was not only in the actualization of a possibility from a number of finite possibilities that man was to reverberate God in understanding but from generating possible realities that reverberate God from the actualization of a possibility in understanding, from understanding, by understanding, and through understanding. We must now look at the understanding of man that is the man, for as previously stated in former books in this series and in this: beings are their understanding. We are as we understand, and as we understand, so we become if that which we understand we, by understanding, integrate to ourselves. There is a way that men, generic, were created and a way that men became after creation; with that way in which there were created being original intent and the former being besides original intent, that is to say, corrupt. By that then, we understand, seeing that men (generic) are their understanding, that their understanding changed after the fall, which is after their corruption. We change when our understanding changes.

As to the change mentioned above: man was in the image and likeness of God, and as such their understanding was in the image and likeness of God, there was in their understanding and through their understanding the reverberation of God, and this not of themselves but from God Who gave. We, therefore, do not reverberate God by virtue of having an understanding but by virtue of having an understanding that is from Him and one that is conformed to His through communion with Him by the acceptance of Jesus Christ as Lord and Savior of our lives. For as it was at the beginning, so it became through Christ; man (generic) was restored to the reverberation of the understanding of God to will as God would through God and not by virtue of having that understanding that is of Christ but by being led by the Spirit of Christ; for even in flesh, with that mind that is a reverberation of God, the second Adam reverberated God by virtue of being led by Him. He said of Himself and pertaining to His works; "...the Son, Christ, can do nothing of Himself but that which He sees the Father do so He does in like manner." All these were due to communion with the Father, and as such was the first Adam, and as such were all that were to be from the first Adam to be being in him, that was humanity and in whom humanity was in. But by virtue of the forbidden fruit, the becoming process of man as it relates to the reverberation of God and the generation of realities reflective of God and the possibilities therein through the development of their understanding in God was lost in Adam. For man became dead, with all that were in him. We see then, that there was not only a death of the man from being separated from God, but the death of Godlike possibilities and their actualization therein, and the generation of invisible kin possibilities from the aforementioned visible possibilities, that is to say, actualized ones. He became contrary to original intent, and yet this becoming was a possibility in the actualized reality in Eden which was the best and perfect possible reality from a variety of innumerable infinite possible realities in the Infinite One, which was fully known by the Infinite One and not only that possibility but the possibilities that would result from the actualization of that possibility by man which was the worst possible reality, as per the best perfect actualized possible reality, and in His sovereign understanding, God actualized the best perfect possible reality from the worst possible reality actualized by man from the best perfect possible reality He had actualized in the person of Christ who died at the cross for the remission of our sins, that is to say, for the regeneration and rebirth of the man in Him, through Him, by Him, and from Him, in Whom all men are and through Whom, all men are as He is as there were in the first Adam. It is, therefore, in the second Adam, that man is restored to the original intent of God, with the possibility of the worst possible reality, which was actualized by the first Adam, remains as a possibility, and yet also as a reality from which man, humanity, was redeemed from being born in it having existed in it in the first Adam. As such, man (generic), is in a reality where these two possibilities have the same probability of actualization, as it were in the beginning, though man is born in the worst possible reality that was actualized by the first Adam. Yet, the worst possible reality is not so much so as it ought to be due to the grace and mercy of the Infinite One, whose Spirit refrains, through Christ's death and His presence, the actualization, of the worst possible reality in its true vein which shall be actualized in the reign of the antichrist.

Chapter 3

ANACHRONISTIC REALITIES

"There is a way that seems right to a man,

But its end is the way of death." Proverbs 14:12 NKJV

The possible reality actualized by Adam in the garden of Eden, which was the worst possible reality from the best and most perfect possible reality actualized by God, introduced anachronisms into his reality by virtue of the sinful nature and that enemy of old, Satan, whom man agreed within his son, allowing him to have access to his reality and the times inherent therein and the time in which that reality exists in. Time and the times therein because man's reality was created from within the time-frequency and is contained in the time-frequency from which all things in it happen at a point in time, and in a season, as witnessed and demonstrated by God Himself who acted in time from a moment in eternity past at each and every single day of creation. It is from these workings of God in time that we understand that time was appointed for appointments, in other words, time is a tool with appointed realities and with realities to be appointed with the appointed realities referring to the times and seasons of our lives that are set and were set on God in a moment in eternity past. As it is written: all the days of my life were written even before any of them were. Moses also speaks of this truth and from this truth when he states: teach us to

10

number our days so that we may gain a heart of wisdom. This heart of wisdom to refer to a heart that knows how to make most of the time allocated for it in the physical realm which necessitates a discerning heart that understands the times and seasons and is able to discern the times and seasons in one's life; the result of which is wise living and gaining such a heart by increasing in understanding. For to the wise and with the wise there is an increase of knowledge through understanding and by an increase of and in understanding. Such a heart writes the reality appointed for the right time and by that virtue avoids the generation of anachronistic realities, which are realities besides their time and season therein. The effects are a ripple effect that generates possible anachronistic realities: for a generated reality generates possible realities, whether anachronistic or not. When an anachronistic reality has been generated, one exists in an anachronistic reality and it takes discernment to generate, from the anachronistic reality, the best possible reality. This takes the working of the Spirit of God in man and a revelation from the Spirit of God in order to avoid the generation of the possible anachronistic realities which vary in effects as it relates to destiny and the number of days allocated for the person on earth. Whatever, we generate can diverge from destiny and can result to premature death for in order for the enemy to kill steal, and destroy, he must generate a reality where these realities are possible and the place where they are possibilities is in the anachronistic realities that we actualize and or those that the enemy causes us to actualize through essokinesis (reality manipulation). The reality we generate because, whatever we actualize that is beside God and His will is anachronistic in nature and generates anachronistic realities which are works of the flesh (sinful nature); it is our sinful nature that generates anachronistic realities because the flesh is enmity with God and does not, and cannot, generate God's ordained reality for us (God's perfect will). Such was the case with the children of Israel who spent 49 years in the desert due to disobedience and lack of faith. It was their lack of faith to possess the land that resulted in that generation not walking into their inheritance at the right time (they didn't actualize God's perfect will). Now, they didn't actualize His perfect will because this actualizes God's perfect will in our lives, we need to have faith and to use faith, which is the evidence of the things hoped for, and the substance of the things not seen. These things hoped for are those that have been spoken to us through prophecy and other means of revelation such as dreams, visions, and so forth. When such is not mixed with faith, the ordained reality is not generated and men exist in anachronistic realities, with an inherent danger of generating the worst possible realities from anachronisms, which would rationally speaking, be worse than the one from which they have been actualized from; which are the minefield of Satan, as previously established in this chapter. By that virtue, Satan, his agents, and demons work at generating anachronistic realities which are of the following types:

1. Church anachronistic realities
2. National anachronistic realities
3. Personal anachronistic realities
4. Family anachronistic realities (generated from the former)
5. Organizational anachronistic realities

Without an agreement with him, there is no generation of anachronistic realities. Discernment is critical to knowing the times and learning to walk according to the times which is by the word that reveals the present time, and the necessitated action as per the working of the Holy Spirit through the believer and in the believer via the word and through the word.

"Your word is a lamp to my feet and a light to my path.", Psalm 119:105 NKJV

Chapter 4

RELATIONSHIPS & POSSIBLE REALITIES

"And the LORD God said, "It is not good that man should be alone; I will make him a helper comparable to him." Genesis 2:18NKJV

Relationship is a dimension in man and a dimension of man by virtue of being in the image and likeness of God, who is relationship and is in the relationship. It is from this dimension of humanity, that men actualize relationships, that is to say, communion and associations with one another, which are in and of themselves possible realities to be actualized; for we will whom to befriend, and likewise who marry from a number of people with different realities that contain different possible realities in them. The union of two persons is thus the unification of two realities with the inherent possibilities therein. We must, therefore, understand that every relationship, which is an actualized possibility, comes with possibilities that have probable actualization and these possibilities are trusted to the one with whom we choose to befriend and or marry. Relationships are possibility actualizers and or possibility killers and God uses people to bring into actualization certain possibilities in us and also uses people to kill certain possibilities in us. The right person will actualize the right possibilities through the aid of the

Spirit, and the wrong person will kill the right possibilities and introduce anachronisms in our reality making our reality an anachronistic reality. We must, therefore, grasp that the person we decide to be with, in friendship and marriage, is one with whom and to whom we trust our possible realities that are inherent in our reality. And since these persons come with different spiritual realities with different spiritual possible realities inherent in them, there is, in the relationships, a merging of spiritual realities and or an engagement of the spiritual realities that causes and creates possible spiritual realities in the relationship that are either-or, in the sense of good or bad. Friendships and marriage are not simply a matter of enjoyment and fun but a matter of creating realities from which certain possible realities, that would otherwise not become, become. It is therefore imperative that we gauge with the Spirit of God and decide with the Spirit of God having been led by the same Spirit whom we are to befriend and whom we are to marry. For there is an association of realities, and the probabilities inherent therein, in the friendship and in marriage. The two, are in and of themselves, actualized possibilities. In His sovereign plan, God has given us the capacity and ability to construct realities through understanding, in understanding, by understanding, from understanding, and for understanding, and for His glory. Now, for understanding is for peace and for walking together into the reality we create as friends and husband and wife, with the latter of cause carrying greater weight in construction, and the former also with its own great weight due to the truth that both affect each other to some and to some degree. It is for this reason that it is written "how can two walk together unless they agree?" That is to say, how can a relationship be constructed unless there is an agreement that has preceded it? The agreement being of soul content, destiny, and of spiritual realities; though not all of the agreements are converged. For there are friendships where there is an agreement of soul content but not an agreement of destiny and or of spiritual realities. Neither is that always the case in marriage, the result of which is oftentimes or not, divorce and or heartache in marriage and it is for this reason that one must discern when choosing friends and choosing marriage partners. For if there is no compatibility, there will be difficulties that may be, and often are said to be, irreconcilable. It is not enough to have a similarity in soul content, and neither is it enough to have an agreement of destiny, it is enough that all three be converged. Of the first, soul content, we just grasp that it doesn't mean that the two just have the same likes and or the same taste in movies, books and so forth or be of the same personality and temperament. It is far from that, it has to do with an agreement of virtue and morals. Similarities in likes and personality and taste do not mean there is a convergence of soul content. It is the morals and principles that dictate human function, and they also are the ones that determine human associations. Virtue then, and an agreement of it in persons is the most significant in terms of soul content and not merely such things as taste and so forth. We must, therefore, see past taste, likes, and so forth to the morals of the individual. Not that likes and such do not matter rather that they are secondary to virtue which is primary and the hinge that makes living and associating with someone pleasant and or contrary. Likes and taste are good, but if we go by them alone and not by virtue, if we do not see past them, we err in section making when it comes to friends. Indeed, it is so! As it is written, bad company ruins good morals. The word of good emphatically speaks of virtues as the most important traits in person's rather that likes and such, which are not at all mentioned in the word of God. A way for the good Lord to tell us to see past them to virtue. It is these virtues that determine which realities are to be actualized and the reality that one is in and the possible realities therein.

We must also understand that an agreement in virtue is not an agreement in spiritual reality! Many have good virtues but are dead spiritually, and those alive spiritually do not have the same spiritual reality and, therefore, have a difference in spiritual activities. Just as virtue determines activities, spiritual realities determine spiritual activities and morally good doesn't mean spiritual alive and spiritually alive doesn't mean spiritually growing. There are those that are spiritually alive but carnal and the possibilities inherent in them are as they are, carnal. Of those that are spiritually alive, there are those that are spiritually growing and have grown to a dimension and a level therein that is of sons and as it would be an incompatible marriage for a son, a grown man in the physical, to marry a child, it would also, in the same way, be incompatible for a spiritual son to marry a spiritual child. While one may contend that the son will mature the child, we need to understand that the spiritual activities of the two are different and the dangers for the child, spiritually speaking, are high due to the marriage and likewise also for the son who is one with them. In like manner also, it is an incompatible marriage for a spiritual son to marry one that is carnal. For the carnal one is still fleshly in thought and the realities therein are of the flesh and not of the Spirit. The result, therefore, will be conflicting realities in the marriage and in the relationship; for one constructs in the Spirit and another in the flesh. One speaks in the Spirit and another in the flesh. One understands by the Spirit and another by the flesh. One is a friend of the world and therefore in enmity, as it were, with God and another is set apart from the world, and by that act is setting themselves apart from the world. Evidently, conflict is assured in the spiritual world and in the physical. Beyond all else, we must know that virtue and likes are immaterial! With the former being in the surface of the immaterial and the latter being in the deep of the immaterial with spiritual reality being the depths of the immaterial of the material person. It is thus categorical to see past the two levels of the person and see into the third level, the depths, of the person. Not the surface, nor the intermediate deep, but the deeps of the person, which is their spiritual reality from whence the reality of the person lies and the possible realities therein. For as our spirits are, so we construct and as our spirits are so are we. There is no place where seeing into the depths of the person is so significant than in the decision of who to marry. For in and of itself marriage is a reality to be constructed, progressively, from having chosen, either by your own counsel or the Lord's, one with whom you are to construct it with. Chosen because there are many women to choose from in relation to the man and many men to choose from in relation to the woman, that is, there are different possible marriage realities to be constructed with their own proceeding realities which have their own proceeding realities both of which are probable prior to the choosing; for as previously stated, different people come with different realities that will be actualized which contain different probable realities.

Chapter 5

UNDERSTANDING & POSSIBILITY

"For as he thinks in his heart, so is he." Proverbs 23:7 NKJV

We are our understanding. As a man thinks so is he. Thinking is a function of understanding, it is a by-product of it. We think because we understand and understand because we think. Now, thinking is a process that produces thought and the thought that is produced is the reality that is crafted in mind in actuality. It is while thinking that possibilities are generated. But not all men generate the same possibilities. As men are distinct so are their understanding. We understand differently because understanding is dimensional and has levels within the dimensions (this is because man is a becoming being, and becomes dimensionally and as previously stated; men are their understanding and it is their understanding that becomes which is who they are). As a result, men generate from what they have understood from their thinking process in the level that they are in within the dimension they are in. It is from that reality that they generate possibilities, that reality because the level and dimension that one is in in their understanding is a reality that was actualized and as such was a possibility that became. Understanding and growth in understanding is a possibility that needs to be actualized. This means that every time and season within the time has its appointed dimension of understanding and level of understanding as per the person's becoming process, which is in times and seasons. This means that when men are not as they ought to be in a time and in a season within the time, their understanding is anachronistic. They are an anachronistic reality as per their becoming process and the time and season therein. We, therefore, see that to avoid anachronistic realities one must be becoming in understanding. If we fail to develop our understanding (that is, become in understanding), we fail to become as per the times and seasons. It is this becoming of understanding and in understanding that generates realities appointed for the times and seasons that we are in. To grow in understanding is to grow in reality generation. The greater our understanding becomes the better the realities to be generated and the possible realities therein. There is a variance in possible realities as per our understanding of the realities we generate. It is this variance that Paul refers to in scripture when he states: "...when I was a child I reason like a child..." Reasoning like a child results in crafting a reality like a child based on one's understanding, which by virtue of the chapter hitherto is a child's actualizing, the best possible reality. We must perceive that all actualized realities are the best possible realities as per one's understanding (the dimension and level therein). There are, however, different types of understanding which are due to man's trichotomous nature, though the understanding is trichotomous in nature.

1. Natural Understanding
2. Spiritual understanding

1. Natural Understanding

"As for these four young men, God gave them knowledge and skill in all literature and wisdom; and Daniel had understanding in all visions and dreams." Daniel 1:17 NKJV

Men (generic) is a composite being: soul, spirit, and body. They relate to the natural world, the physical realm, with natural Understanding which is appointed for grasping natural things. This natural understanding is a dimension in their understanding. It is this that God increased in Daniel, Shadrach, Meshach, and Abednego so that they can understand the literature and culture of the Babylonian. Without this dimension of our understanding, we cannot grasp the natural world and matters relating to the natural world such as science and technology, and the elementary principles of this realm that are contained in the natural sciences which are taught in school for the sole purpose of developing this dimension of our understanding which is critical in developing character, soul content. It is, arguably, from education that men have developed and tapped into the potential of their natural understanding, which is a gift from God. Now, this understanding is developed by men naturally, i.e., by learning things that relate to this realm and the affairs of this realm.

2. Spiritual Understanding

"...that the God of our Lord Jesus Christ, the Father of glory, may give to you the spirit of wisdom and revelation in the knowledge of Him." Ephesians 1:17 NKJV

Spiritual things cannot be understood naturally but by spiritual understanding, which is a dimension of man's understanding that is given and was given to man for the understanding of things that are spiritual and of the spiritual realm that is beyond the physical realm of man. God is spirit, and He is understood via spiritual intelligence. Before the fall, man had both understandings functioning in their full capacity as per the dimension of understanding man was in in the respective dimensions of understanding and the levels therein. Spiritual things became foreign to man through the corruption of his understanding and that of those in him, that is all of mankind which was in Adam. Through Christ, and in Christ, the natural and spiritual intelligence are restored in Him via His Spirit, that resides in us in Whom and through Whom we reside in Christ Jesus and are in Him Who is in

God the Father. Christ then came to restore both understandings in man which are characteristics of the abundant life, which is what was at the beginning and in the beginning as it was in Eden in Christ, and through the Spirit in Christ.

Now, we need to understand that both understandings, which are dimensions of the mind of man, are for the construction and deconstruction of physical and spiritual realities that man is part and parcel of. Without the harmonic convergence of both, and the working of both, men cannot construct the reality appointed for them and the possible realities therein. We see, then that sin caused a separation, a lack of harmony between the two dimensions of the mind of man, which as previously stated is restored in Him that is God in flesh. The plan of Satan involved both the dimensions of man's understanding to cause man and all men (generic) in him to fall. As it is written:

"... When the woman saw…":

1. The tree was good for food

2. Pleasing to the eye

3. Desirable to make man wise

"...she took it and she ate it, and gave some to her husband that was with her."

Saw to mean, reasoned using her understanding through which she saw it was good for food, would meet a natural need, pleasing to the eye, aesthetically pleasing, physically speaking it was of physical form and in physical form, and desirable to make one wise: as God, a corrupt spiritual desire which was in spiritual understanding. The natural and the spiritual dimensions of man's understanding were corrupt at the fall and as such, the reality to flow from them were likewise corrupt. For, corruption of nature is a corruption of understanding, and as a result, of the thinking process, both spiritual and physical. It is from understanding that reality and the possible realities reside. As it is written:

"As a man thinks so is he." Proverbs 23:7 NKJV

As men understand they become and as they become they construct. It is in understanding that we become. The development of both understandings causes us to become and we become to do, that is: we become to construct. But if our understanding has been affected through pain, heartache, sorrow, and grief: what we become becomes contrary to the original intent and to be restored one must be cleansed by the blood of the Lamb. It is in the cleansing of understanding that we become according to original intent and author realities and possible realities according to original intent.

26

Chapter 6

IMAGINATION

"...the imagination of man's heart..." Genesis 8:21 NKJV

Imagination is a faculty of mind responsible for image perception and image generation. It is the imagination that sees through the eye. When we think of what can be and what should be or what we deem is to be, we see it in our imagination as we would want it to be. And as such were all the infinite possible realities in the imagination of God. He saw them in Him and saw all the possible realities from all the possible infinite possibilities of how creation could be like. He also, along with the mentioned, saw the reality He intended to construct with all its possible realities prior to its actualization and all of man's possible realities in Eden, and all possible realities from Eden as a result of eating the fruit and as a result of not eating the fruit. He, therefore, saw the possible possibilities of Adam, those of Eve, and those of Eve and Adam and those of humanity in Adam with each person's possible realities from the best possible reality He had actualized and from the worst possible reality that Adam could have actualized, and actualized. All these from that genesis of creation in eternity past. When it, therefore, reads: on the beginning, God created the heavens and the earth, which is to say when God had constructed and deconstructed reality in Himself and saw it in Himself, He saw all realities, those possible and those that would be possible from those that man and angels would actualize, within the two constructed realms (primary reality). The fall, of man and Satan, alike were known before they happened, and all that would follow were known and not that God would not prevent them from happening, He would and could have; but love demand free will and man (generic) and angels were created in the image and likeness of God, Who is free and is with free will to will as He decides through His understanding and on His understanding as per His nature which is good. And so, man (humanity) was also good and all angels were good and could will from this good and in this good, which was from God and could only be in God and not be beside Him. Both could, as a consequence, will that which is good because they were good, but being good, in the sense of beings, means being free to choose and not only that which is good but that which is contrary to good and contrary to God and the goodness from God, which Satan willed to do from his goodness, corrupting his goodness by desiring to be the Good which is the Goodness of all good on account of his given goodness that he saw as his own rather than as one that is given. Seeing it as his own, rather than a given grace, though his own but not of himself; he desired to be God (and this from freewill which is good and from God's goodness). As a consequence, he became evil and through this evil deceived woman to actualize a reality that would be in agreement with him from the goodness (freewill) given to her. Not that the good, freewill, brought about evil, rather that the good was corrupt and brought about evil by the decision to reject the good. Freewill is a reality constructor. Satan constructed willingly what he knew was wrong. He understood and knew the truth but neglected it and rejected it. The more he neglected it, the more he became contrary to original intent. Eventually, he left his abode and blessed state in the blessed place.

God could have stopped all these, but having willed to have men and angels have free will, he opted, as a function of His divine will, which necessitated that man and angels have free will, to construct from the best possible reality from the worst possible reality that would be actualized by both. He allows it to play out as He saw it in eternity past, prior to the reality of angels and men or reveal His wisdom, love, and power which was intended to be known by them in the most blessed of states in the most blessed of places (communion with God). He works through the imperfect to reveal His perfect nature. This working, was constructed before the foundations of the earth were laid, that is: the conception of creation and the perceiving of the possibilities that would be actualized and the possibilities that would be birthed within the actualized possibilities was with a certain plan, that was not a possibility but an actuality prior to the aforementioned possibilities, that was to be actualized and was actualized in eternity past awaiting manifestation in time. For, on the seventh day God finished all of His works, which include the work redemption which is what actualized at the cross and is being actualized in time having been actualized in God in eternity past beyond Genesis 1:1. In God, Christ was slain and in Him, man is restored to the reality of Eden and the possibilities in Eden to construct possibilities reflective of God through their own imagination, that are redeemed in Christ and through Christ. All of history was, therefore, conceived prior to its genesis with all the possible possibilities and their possible possibilities and them with their possible possibilities and so forth and on till the end of history. This, however, does not mean that we do not have free will rather that we have it and that he knows all that we can will and will decide to actualize as a possibility and as a loving Father, He directs us to the best possible possibility which we still have to will to actualize; for one can reject guidance as much as they can accept it, and that He knows what we will accept and reject doesn't hinder Him from leading us and guiding us. The most wonderful expression and demonstration of love. This leading is through imagination and in imagination as much as it is in understanding through the small still voice; for it is written: your sons and daughters shall have visions. That is, shall have realities projected through their imagination and in their imagination for actualization, warning, and guidance. In essence, visions are projections of realities that are ordained and those that are possible from the ordained and those that are possible from those that are not ordained but from those that are constructed by men from their own understanding as was the case with Adam and Eve. We see that there is a forecast from God in the imagination of men and through the imagination of men. Even besides God's usage of the imagination, the imagination of man is for forecasting. Men imagine (see) what they desire and what they are to be in their imagination before they are that very thing and or have the thing that is desired (men - generic - construct their realities in imagination and perceive the possible realities in the imagination through imagination and then will which reality to construct). This is to mean that men project realities in their imagination. What they generate through imagination they project through imagination, by imagination, in imagination, and from imagination; actualizing it as a reality in themselves and then from themselves. The actualization of reality in the self, precedes actualization of reality from the self. This was the case with God Who actualized, through imagination and understanding in Himself and through Himself and by Himself in and by His imagination and through the same, projecting creation in Himself prior to projecting it from Himself (which is the actualization of creation from Him having been actualized in Him).

Chapter 7

SOUL CONSTRUCTION

"The eye is not satisfied with seeing,

Nor the ear filled with hearing."

Ecclesiastes 1:8 NKJV

It is the soul that sees through the eye and the soul that hears through the ear and as such the soul develops in its content through what it hears and sees. The soul is ever receiving but doesn't ever get full. In essence, the soul reverberates the law of Infinity in its function. As a consequence, the soul has infinite potential as it relates to its faculties. There is no limit to what man can understand, to what can be recalled, to what can be seen, what can be constructed, and, doubtless, there is no limit to what the soul can construct nor the construction of the soul. It is ever under construction through what it receives, understands, and sees. It is the aforementioned that are in truth what construct the soul. As such; the physical senses are appointed for an accumulation of the physical realm with the dimension of man's understanding that is physical, so to speak, in the sense that it is appointed to grasp the natural, being a decipher and interpreter of the physical realm. The soul is, therefore, a constructor of secondary reality as per the understanding of the natural dimension of the mind. But the soul is constructed prior to its constructing. The soul does not construct unless it is constructed. How it is constructed determines how it constructs. In truth: the soul was constructed to be constantly constructed and as such it is ever under construction with the genesis taking place at conception. The moment there is life in the womb, there is construction in the womb. The becoming process begins in the womb as it relates to the three dimensions of man. It is for this reason that many have grown with rejection having been rejected while in the womb. Words spoken over the child in formation construct the reality of the child while in the womb which means that what we speak over them constructs their soul content in that the faculties can be limited and or interfered with in terms of their functionality and potential; for where there is a function there is potential. Souls are, as previously stated, with infinite potential which is due to their reverberation of Eternity and thence their working through and in the reverberation of the law of infinity which as per the word, the scripture of the chapter, is the law by which the ear and eye function but it is not the law through which and in which the ability of the soul to recall functions. The soul receives without limitation but does not access without limitation. There is, due to sin, a lack of harmony of the soul with itself. The capacity and ability of the soul are out of harmony. Without a harmonic convergence of capacity and ability, the soul does not mirror God as intended. The reverberation of God in the soul is not as was before the fall. Men do not forget what they know, they fail to access what they know and it is this failing to access what they know, that is termed as forgetting. In truth: man was not created to forget. Man's was not to forget. We began forgetting when Adam fell and we in him and by that virtue became like him in him, in whom we were. We began to reverberate the fallen man in an inharmonious state with himself and God. His corrupt faculties became our own in him and through him. This means that the soul's potential to construct is not entirely used and that the soul's construction is faulty due to faulty soul construction in Adam. All souls were reconstructed in Adam through sin and in sin. This deconstruction resulted in man failing to construct his soul as intended because we construct our souls as we learn and in learning. It is indeed true that we are what we learn and also true that we are not all we have learned because we cannot access all that we have learned nor has that which we have learned been assimilated into the soul through the soul via the will, understanding, and memory in its entirety. But that it has not been integrated to the soul entirely tells that there is an integration in some degree that has formed, as it were, the soul and its content which in effect constructs the possibilities in the soul and from the soul. In the soul, because there is a precede of a soul reality before there is a proceeding of reality from the soul and this precede of the soul reality is not without possibilities for the soul that is, is with Possibilities. Whatever is, has possibilities by virtue of existing, and by that truth: the soul's existence is with possibilities. Adam was constructed as a soul with possibilities. In essence, men are an actualized possibility with possibilities to actualize in them and through them. But there are only two possibilities of what the soul can be that are coupled with possibilities akin to the two possibilities of what the soul can be. That is, there are two types of possibilities of what the soul can be and kinds of possibilities within the types of possibilities of what the soul can be inherent the two types of possibilities and there are in the kinds of possibilities kinds within kinds of possibilities of what the soul can be within the kinds of possibilities in the two types of possibilities. It is for this reason that men are given over to certain evils and not others. The soul, that gives itself to sin, will however die; for all evil must die and all evil will die in the second death after the coming of Christ Who comes and will come to actualize the possibility of divinity in humanity and humanity in divinity, the Christian reality that is characterized with and in sinlessness and eternal blessedness in the Divine Creator and Divine God Whom man was created to reverberate and communion with endlessly.

Now, it is imperative to know that the soul actualizes a reality that suits it and accommodates its own reality. We construct realities based on how we have constructed our souls. As we are so we do. We do to be as we are and to become as we are, in the sense of desire. For a desire is something in us that is and is part of us being in us but not us being part of us but not us and being so, we actualize a possibility that will accommodate the consumption of our desires, which are part of the soul but not the soul; and the soul is not without. As was with Eve who desired the fruit and actualizes the reality of the consumption of the fruit, a possibility that accommodates the consumption of her desire. Yet, this consummation was preceded by reasoning about the fruit and the possible reality it contained: "...you will be like God." And not in the sense of the reverberation of God, which was their reality, and that of all in Adam, but be like God in that they will be God. The fruit contained the reality of being God, so said Satan to them; and it was from that desired reality, which included the rejection of their own nature and the rejection of God as God that the man and woman, deconstructed their souls and the reality and possibilities inherent in their sinless state. From good, and hence, good possibilities and good state - good soul content (Genesis 1:31)- to bad and corrupt and therefore bad and corrupt soul states, and evil and corrupt possibilities (Jeremiah 17:9-10). It is in the deconstruction and construction of the soul that the man realizes the potential inherent in them. It is for this reason that Christ died: to restore man to that blessed state and the blessed ...

possibilities inherent in the blessed state with these blessed state and blessed Possibilities requiring and necessitating a restoration of the reality of the soul's faculties that are responsible for the construction of the reality of the soul and that of the reality from the soul. We see then, that in the blessed state of Adam, prior to the fall, and of the second Adam besides the fall and after the fall, in as far as Christ is man, contains an actualized possible reality of the soul and its faculties that reverberate God as intended. The memory without forgetting, understanding without struggle or limitation, imagination without limitation. Man was of noble mind and of noble possibilities that reverberated infinity, from which the possibilities to be actualized were reflective of the nature of God. The soul was not only to reverberate God in capacity but also in ability. As such the realities to be constructed and the possibilities therein were to be great beauty and glory; and yet not besides God nor greater in beauty than He. In truth: we have not yet seen the actualization of many possibilities due to the truth that man's understanding is still not as intended. For in all things constructed it is the mind that constructs and in the growth of understanding and from the growth of understanding, by accessing dimensions of understanding in Christ and through Christ and from Christ being in Christ and having been born of Christ and set free from sin, man will construct, in that age to come such as was intended. And not to mean that now, in

Christ, and from Christ and by Christ, and through Christ in Whom we have the reverberation of the divine mind, man cannot construct possibilities that are great and beautiful. We can in Him and through Him but still in Him and through Him, there are dimensions of understanding we shall access in communion and sinless perfection through His Spirit, by His Spirit, and in His Spirit Who even now deconstructs and constructs our minds to the image and likeness of God for the construction of God like possibilities. That is possibilities that reverberate God from the actualization of a soul reality that reverberates God though the second in Christ and through Him.

"And do not be conformed to this world, but be transformed by the renewing of your mind *(let your soul's reality and state be made new as it was intended in original intent)*, that you may prove what is that good and acceptable and perfect will of God." Romans 12:2 NKJV

Chapter 8

REJECTION & SOUL CONSTRUCTION

"For God knows that in the day you eat of it your eyes will be opened, and you will be like God, knowing good and evil."

Genesis 3:5 NKJV

A statement laden with deception and clothed with a plot to cause man to reject himself, and desire to be something other than what they were created to be and become which in agreeing with; humanity desired to be God rather than be humanity. And so we see that the first rejection was not from humanity to humanity by humanity through humanity. It is this, that was coupled with the lust of the eyes, the pride of life, and the desire of the flesh; for in looking at the fruit, it was good for food, pleasant to the eye, and able to make one wise (wise as in the sense of exactly as God which is to be God: the rejection of humanity by humanity that introduced rejection to humanity). Indeed, where there has been the rejection of self it has been due to the three things that Eve considered:

1. Good for food (lust of the flesh) - appealing to the appetite of the body and or not appealing to it

2. Pleasant to the eye (lust of the eyes) - the desire of the beautiful, to be as beautiful as another, to be like

another in appearance, rejecting our own appearance and rejecting another due to their appearance

3. Able to make one wise (pride of life) - be more knowledge, to have theoretical wisdom and practical wisdom like another, to reject another due to their lack of the aforementioned, and reject ourselves due to our lack of the aforementioned in comparison with and to another

Self-rejection is a consequence of rejection and consistent comparison either by being compared to someone else by another person or by comparing oneself to someone else which results to the altering of the soul's constitution in an attempt to configure oneself to another's image and likeness- which is in truth rejecting the image and likeness of God that is engraved in being ourselves from whence we become like Him being made new in Him - by accepting Christ- and through Him from Whom we are and in Whom we are called to be and live in and through and by being made for Him and through Him to reverberate Him which we cannot do when we try to be like someone else by rejecting who we are which in turn causes frequency demodulation and cognitive dissonance whose consequence is personality alteration and unhealthy soul reconstitution that reconstructs the soul's reality changing the probable realities in the soul and from the soul. For when the soul is changed, it's reality is changed and with its change, there is a change of the realities in the soul, the faculties and personality - which is in the soul through self-abandonment. One cannot desire to be like another and not abandon themselves and it is this that causes mental dissonance that affects the reception of information, the functioning of understanding in grasping and comprehending, and perception of reality, what is known as a worldview; for to adapt be in the image and likeness of another is to reconstitute oneself to the other, that is; to become a reverberation of another rather than of God. Man was not created to reverberate another but to reverberate God. Yes. It is true that children are reverberations of their parents, but only in as much as it relates to being human and such as are the reverberations in them through the DNA and the information in the blood. But they are not to be them, they are to be themselves. And so it was that Adam had a son in his own image and likeness, but the son was not him but a reverberation of his humanity through birthing. It is through birthing and in birthing that we reverberate humanity and likewise, through being birthed in God, through God, by God and from God, and in God, we reverberate God. As such, when we aim to be like another rather than be ourselves and reconstitute our soul through frequency modulation we are attempting to birth ourselves through the person we want to be like which causes the loss of ourselves. We, in the spirit, make them our "parents", so to speak. We are birthed again, through ourselves, in them, by them, from them, and to them. To them because whatever is birthed from is birthed to. What is born of God is birthed to God, and what is born of men is birthed for men. We make ourselves their reverberation by rejecting our person, changing our reality and inviting the enemy to manipulate our reality, as it was in the fall. Humanity rejected itself, opening themselves up and their reality to manipulation by the enemy due to the truth that self-rejection involves the rejection of one's internal (spiritual and soul reality) and external reality, secondary reality, which is a by-product of the former: Rejecting the former is a rejection of the latter which is a rejection of the actualized inherent reality, and the possibilities therein and the actualized secondary reality and the possibilities therein. One cannot reject themselves and not reject them because they are a by-product of who they are. It is for this reason that there is mental dissonance, a conflict of who one is and who one wants to be that they were never called and or created to be and become.

Now, as a consequence of the aforementioned, the becoming process and the realities of the person as per their times and seasons are altered. Who they ought to be at a time and the season in the time they do not become. The alignment between heaven and them is absent. Your will be done on earth as it is in heaven is tampered with because God's will for us involves being ourselves. It is in being us that we partner with the Holy Spirit and become like Him through Whom we are and have become to become like Him whose plan for us we reject in rejecting ourselves. We cannot fulfil destiny in self-rejection and self-comparison. We are to learn from others, and only as far as it will enable us to reverberate God, but not be others nor be in their image and likeness as in the aforementioned sense of being born through them and in them (yet we are born of God to reverberate Him). Destiny requires authentic selves not copies of others. Our timelines require us to be originals not photocopies. When our personalities are rejected, the realities we are to construct from our person change and we desire to construct the realities which are like those of the person's we want to be. Our lives begin to follow their pattern. Developed disciplines are abandoned, morals and principles are altered and as such, the probabilities we actualize and those that we create. In truth: self-rejection and the resulting soul reconstitution is a testament of how the fall of humanity in Adam brought insecurity to who and what we are, which was the genesis of the fall also involved our personalities. The personality of man must be redeemed in Him, being constructed from Him and being a reverberation of Him that is our lives. If we are to, therefore, reverberate Him, our personalities must be redeemed through the Holy Spirit and in the Holy Spirit that He may reconstitute our personality by modulating our frequencies and restoring personality back to original intent.

Chapter 9

THE BEGINNING OF REJECTION

"For you (Satan) have said in your heart:

I will ascend into heaven,

I will exalt my throne above the stars of God;

I will also sit on the mount of the congregation

On the farthest sides of the north..." Isaiah 14:3 NKJV

Satan desired to be God. Wanted to be God and by that act rejected himself and desired to be something other than what he was created to be. It is this that is the beginning of rejection. It was in eternity past that rejection began. Before man became rejection was and before rejection became in man it had become before man in Satan who deceived a third of the heavens and caused them to reject themselves and reject God by desiring to be more than they had been made to be. They, therefore, became less than they had been created to become and as it was through the pride of life, the lust of the eyes, and the lust of the flesh that humanity rejected humanity, so it was that Satan rejected himself and the rest with him rejected themselves. For it is written: by the abundance of his trading he became violent within. Now, the abundant of his trading refers to his duty and task in the heavens as a service to God which involved wisdom, knowledge, and understanding, music and the various types and kinds within the types and kinds within the kinds of sounds which are the pride of life, and on account of his beauty he was lifted up; the lust of the eyes, and his desire to take the place of God and be God; the pride of life and the lust of the eyes for he desired that beauty that was of the divine Creator and the glory of the living God Who is the One and only true God from Whom all beauty precedes and through Whom all things beautiful became in Him and from Him through Him that is the epitome of beauty. Being therefore deceived, Satan took the gift of beauty as his own and not as a gift. Having been given it, he made it his own glory rather than for the glory of the King of all glory. His wisdom was a gift from the Spring of Wisdom but he made it his own as if by himself and through himself he became deconstructing his soul to be besides what it was and what it was created to be, a reverberation of God; he became contrary to original intent and created in himself a reality devoid of God and generated possibilities in himself, through himself, and by himself that were contrary to the good, and were, as it is with everything devoid of God, evil. For evil is whatever is devoid of God and contrary to God. The deconstruction of Satan resulted in the actualization of the worst possible reality from the best possible reality that God had actualized for the angels and Satan as well. Satan actualized the worst possible reality in himself and in others due to deception, and in like manner he deceived man to introduce the worst possible reality from the best possible reality that God had constructed for man which introduced other possible realities akin to the worst possible reality actualized by man. Till this day, Satan actualizes and seeks to actualize, the worst possible realities from the worst possible reality that he actualized in himself and through himself in his spiritual domain and in the physical realm upon which he was given authority by man at the fall; allowing him to construct the reality of the physical realm to his image and likeness, that it may reverberate him though it was created to reverberate God through humanity that was called and created to reverberate God in being and in their domain. Needless to say, Satan changed his vibration charge and energy from negative to positive from which he has become besides what he was created to be.

"All who knew you among the peoples are astonished at you;
You have become a horror,
And shall be no more forever." Ezekiel 28:19 NKJV

Chapter 10

FAITH

"Now faith is the substance of things hoped for, the evidence
of things not seen." Hebrews 11:1 NKJV

Faith integrates man to God's reality and aids man constructs realities ordained by God, in God, for construction in the physical realm through God, and by God in man and through man. It is through faith that man is connected to the possible realities in God and the possible realities within them. Further than being a means of integration through harmonic convergence and in harmonic convergence, faith is a substance: the material by which, in which, and through which what is hoped for is constructed being unseen through and in the physical eye but not being inexistent in word from God or in vision from God through the projection of images in the imagination of man. Being an evidence, it is a witness of what is invisible through the material eye and with the material eye but not necessarily unseen by and with imagination. Yes. It is the imagination that sees through the eye but there are things projected in the imagination by God that must be believed for their actualization. Indeed, the will must submit to the Divine for the realities ordained by the divine to come to pass through the hope that they shall come to be: for hope is based on that which is not but will be. That is, that which is not but is a possibility that can be and has

48

been ordained to be. Can be, because the future is not written in stone. It is appointed to become through the actualization of possibilities that lead to it's becoming. There are probable realities that lead to the actualization of ordained possibilities and these that lead to the actualization of ordained possibilities are also possibilities that are ordained for actualization. There is a ripple effect. A cause and effect that manifests the appointed reality. In truth: God works from our beginning to actualize every reality that will result in the actualization of our appointed reality: what we have been called to become, to do, and the reality we have been called to actualize (destiny) which requires faith in Him Who is the Destiny of destiny. In essence, every destiny contains many realities to be actualized through its actualization in the lives of those that are to benefit from one's destiny and the one to whom the destiny is appointed. There are realities synthetically joined to the reality of one's destiny. These joined realities are to be birthed from the vision of the destiny in those that are to benefit from the vision. For every destiny has beneficiaries that benefit through faith in God. It is through faith in God and in faith in God that the things of God and the destinies appointed us to receive the essence of substantialization.

Gifts, signs, wonders, and all such works of the person of the Holy Spirit through man and in man are for the actualization of the realities appointed by God for man. It is through the works of the Spirit which is by necessity through being in Christ and being in Christ having been drawn by the Father through the conviction of the Holy Spirit Who regenerates our spirits with His creative energy that is in the creation frequency and with the creation frequency, that is the manifestation of the Alpha dimension of God, that these works of God are manifest which are by faith and in faith in God in Whom those that believe are and are used to work the works of God in God. Having been integrated with God and in God by God through faith in God, the realities of God are transmitted through the Spirit of God in man by virtue of the convergence so that there can be the expression of Infinity in humanity and humanity in Infinity (the reverberation of God - what it means to be in the image and likeness of God) for the redemption of mankind. All works of the Spirit are for the crystallization of the appointed realities in the lives of man. And so it was that Christ taught them that believed, had faith in Him through Him to pray: "...Your will be done on earth as it is in heaven." That is: your appointed realities be constructed on earth as they are constructed in heaven. It was those that believed that were taught to actualize realities appointed for crystallization in the physical realm and the possibilities therein. We are, therefore, to actualize possible realities that reflect our faith. In truth: we actualize realities that reflect our theology. As our theology is, so are our mental constructs, the realities we construct in mind and the probabilities that in actualization become our physical constructs, i.e. our secondary reality. One's faith is appointed for soul deconstruction and construction: for the object of our faith determines our anthropology, and sociology (which are the basis of human interaction and engagement: anthropology determines human relations - the realities of our relationships) through the spirit behind the faith, and therefore, in that spirit, by that spirit, and from that spirit. For the Christian, this is through the Spirit of God, and in that Spirit, by that Spirit, from that Spirit and to the glory of God Who is that Spirit and for the good of men by walking in that Spirit and being led by that Spirit Who works in us to actualize God's appointed realities for our souls that changes the possible realities in our souls and the realities we construct and the probabilities produced by them. And so it is that the more we are in communion with the Spirit through the grace of Our Lord Jesus Christ, and by that grace in which we received the Holy Spirit, by the love of God the Father, Whose love is embodied in Christ and His Spirit, that the realities of God grow in us and their manifestations through us in Christ.

Chapter 11

THE REIFICATION PROCESS

(An extract from The Pneumatic Nature of Reality)

"In the beginning, God created the heavens and the earth."

Genesis 1:1 NKJV

"And on the seventh day God ended His work which He had done, and He rested on the seventh day from all His work which He had done. Then God blessed the seventh day and sanctified it, because in it He rested from all His work which God had created and made." Genesis 2:2- 3 NKJV

"God ended His work..." Work is a function of being as per ability directed by counsel which proceeds from the mind of the being, which is home to nature of the being. A deed reveals a dimension of a being whereas deeds reveal the nature of the being. A deed is singular and referentially applies to a particular setting revealing a dimension of the being; deeds, plural, are interdimensional; revealing the nature of the being. A being's revelation being the sum total of its dimensional expressions. Deed reveals a dimension of a being; deeds reveal nature. Deeds are interdimensional, a deed is dimensional. Nature is therefore inter-dimensional but revealed dimensionally. This means that persons are revealed through a deed and deeds. Deed and deeds because a deed reveals the dimension of a person and deeds dimensions of a person. Being, therefore, precedes doing because doing is a work of being. What is not cannot do and what does, does because it is. It does not do to be (exist), it does because it is.

Mind, being home to the nature of being, reveals nature in doing of being. As such we find that counsel which is a product of thinking is what we act upon, what is counsel and is according to nature. We think as we are and therein do as we are having thought as we are. This doing being one that includes speaking which is an act of being as much as thinking is an act of being. Thought, therefore, is a product of an act of being that is cognitive which results in a deed that is without; thinking being a deed of being that is within. Thinking is a work that is innate and in the faculty of mind, that is understanding. A faculty is an ability and therein understanding is the ability to think, grasp, and or make sense of whatever is and or can be or was. What is, to mean what exists, what can be to mean what is possible in existing, and what was to mean what is past and therefore existed. What is possible is from what is, that is to say, that what exists is the cause of what can exist. Therefore, we find that we can only understand what is and not what is not for what was existed, was at some point an is before it became past (that it is past does not mean it did not exist and that it was means it existed), and what 'is' clearly exists and can, therefore, be presently understood from which what can be, that is what can exist, can be understood from what exists. Necessity is the mother of innovation means that what has not been before in time past and is not in time present becomes, that is to say, exists, through a need that is, even what has not been is a product of what is for a need is what is which must be understood to be met in a way that is not or is. Everything is, therefore, a product of what is. Reality births reality. For something to be, there must be a work which is preceded by ability, that is to say, power. Work is a product of an ability (power). This work is the ability to write as in the sense of produce. To work in is to produce from. As one's ability is so is their production. We do as we are able not as we are not or desire to be. Ability, therefore, dictates production. Produce is a reflection of ability.

It is, therefore, in beings to produce. Now, since the ability of being is in being and therefore part of being but not being. Not being because being precedes doing and when being does not do, being still is. So, whether a being does or does not do, being remains being but it is in being to do, that is to produce and, conclusively, it is upon being to produce. Upon because ability is subject to being, being part of being rather than being that which is being. Being works and this that is being causes doing. Having stated that ability is part of being and not being, we find that that which is being is what causes being to do. Ability is not its own master since to do one must direct their doing, as is evident in whatever we, as humans do. Looking back to the genesis of this writing; work which results to produce is as a result of thought, the by-product of understanding. Now, to understand one must will to understand, and to will to understand one must understand that they are willing to understand. Work is, therefore, a product of understanding because to will one must understand. You do as you understand, as much as you will as you understand. Understanding is, therefore, critical to production and willing. It would, by the aforementioned be right to say that to be or to be ending is to understand. Understanding is, therefore, that which is being hence the statement by Rene Descartes: "I think therefore I am." We know we are because we understand. Understanding is what it means to be being and as is the understanding so is the being. Nature of being is therefore as is the understanding.

Understanding is through sound and is in sound. Thinking is the process of using one's sound to reason, that is to say, to understand. To be being is, therefore, to be able to think. Being is therefore sound. Sound because to will we must understand, and to understand we use sound, and that which is understanding is sound. All beings are therefore sound, and understanding is a working of being through itself being that being is sound and sound is the working of the being, and all works from being are therefore as a product of their understanding that is the sound of being and being. Being that being is understanding, ability is directed by understanding. Developing understanding is developing being because being is understanding. As we develop our understanding, that which is being and we do as we understand and or do to understand, in the sense of reasoning - what is innate doing, we find that ability is directed by understanding. Power is developed through understanding and seeing that development of being is through understanding for being is understanding; ability is developed by understanding, in it, through it, and by it.

Into the Process in Eternity Past

To therefore do, use power and therein direct power, better and produce better, we must develop being, and being is understanding. In the sense and respect of the power of God, it is as directed by the being of God, the mind of God and one must know the mind of God to work the works of God. For God is Being of beings, and Understanding of Understanding (as being is understanding), and therein works the "Works of works" being Being of beings. The very term God means Supreme Being and having established being as understanding, we find that the aforementioned about God is true. These "Work of works", are beyond the works of other being and their ability (His ability is "Ability of abilities").

Rendering Him the most powerful Being. What we, therefore, call miracles are these "Works of works". To, therefore, do the works of God, one must grow in the mind of God; that is to say, one must understand God and become as He is for, we become as we understand and what we understand. This becoming as He is is not in exactness but in the reflection of; what is growing in the image and likeness of God which is how we were created to be in and grow in. Becoming like God, what is meant by understanding and growing in the understanding of God, results in the working of the works of God which is out of the understanding of God and therefore in God. In God, because to understand God one must have God in them, which is what is intimacy. Being in God, it is therefore from God, through God, by God, and to God. To God being it is for His glory and not our own. It is so for the work of being is for the glory of being. Work which produces and therein is glory is a revelation of the glory of being. The glory of being is in the produce of being. Produce reveals glory. What man does reveals man's glory. Whatever God does reveals His glory. To, therefore, be used to reveal the Glory of God, one must be led by God by understanding the sound of God for sound is understanding. God is, therefore, Sound of sound being sound. To understand the Sound of sound is to discern the Sound of God which is through the understanding of God acting upon the understanding of man teaching and training Him to understand that of God. What we call discernment is the ability to understand one thing and therein distinguish it from what it is not which is what is, therefore, setting it apart.

The works of God are therefore dependent on the Sound of God. The reason all began with His Sound, John 1:1-3. The works of being, therefore, depend on the understanding of being. The works of God are entirely dependent on the person of God not on man's works but on God's works. It, therefore, takes God to influence God. It takes God to cause God to act. It is God's understanding that does God's work. The frequency of God produces what is of God. Production is therefore in frequency and through frequency. What we, therefore, call power is a movement of frequency dependent on the speed, pace of work, intensity, and or heaviness of the frequency of the being. For every being is frequency and frequency is being. Every being is Pneumatic in nature, that is: is breath and sound (the two being indivisible from each other in essence and substance for they are one; the pneumatic is wind and sound). Now, what that means is that the sound and the breath of God is the means through which God does, the breath and sound of God being God. For one is their sound and their breath. Breath being spirit and sound being a soul in the context of the man. And as God functions, so is the man called to mirror; man, therefore works through their understanding and or frequency and breath with the pace being dependent on the intensity and or heaviness, which is the glory of the frequency and breath that is the person. Glory is therefore in person. A person is their glory, and this glory is inherent in their frequency.

This work(s) being done from the glory of the person(s) is preceded by appointing through conceiving with and in understanding. To therefore work is to write reality. Work is the writing of reality. What we call the works of God are the realities written by God and that which is written is appointed through the mind! This appointing is through reasoning which is for deciding, that is for appointing. Whatever we decide we appoint and what we appoint we do, that is we work out which is to mean we write as a reality. There is, therefore, the process of the writing of reality. The process is an integrational work of the faculties of the mind in the following manner:

1. Intellect thinks about

2. Imagination conceives in a form that which intellect has reasoned and is reasoning about

3. Understanding conceives what it has imagined and thought of for imagination and intellect are faculties that work correspondingly and to understand we must understand that we are understanding and or seeking to understand and to imagine we must understand that we

are imagining; therefore, grasping the idea and the form in the idea

4. Examining through understanding in understanding whether the conceived and the development of the conceived are in agreement and also whether the conceived is according to the design intended from the conception of it in thought and imagination

5. Agree in understanding with the understanding that it is fitting and worth willing therein to say worth producing that is to say worth writing as a reality in which case if it is, it is appointed in mind, from the mind, through the mind, and by the mind, and therefore consequently, produced by the mind for that very mind that has produced it; for we produce a reality agreeable to our minds for our minds which is conclusively a reality that is in our image and likeness

The aforementioned are on account of their integrated nature, and of point 5; the process of creation in mind, through the mind, for the mind, by the mind, and to mind. To mind because reality is produced for the mind and therein is, as previously stated; in the image and likeness of that mind from which it has come through, come from, and became in and through, and has become. Became in because it became in mind, by the mind, before it became from the mind and therein through the mind. Reality, therefore, becomes in mind before it is in reality.

Progressively, it would mean that: We must become in mind before we become in reality (actuality). "As a man thinks so is he.": Which is to mean that as a man has become in mind he becomes in actuality (reality). You don't become what you've been called to be without seeing yourself as it in mind and without becoming it in mind first by agreeing to it (refer to the 5-stage progress of becoming in mind). Now, since what we have agreed to, we appoint and write we must recall it having understood it, for we remember what we have understood having willed to understand it, and must consistently will to remember it from having understood it. Remembering it will keep us in the becoming progress stage that is from the mind, that is to say from mind to reality. We must remember what we have appointed to appoint it. Creation was therefore also a work of God's memory! He appointed it in mind, then called it as He had appointed it in mind but to have appointed it in mind is at a moment in eternity past, as it is a process with each stage having its own moment, and to therefore call it into being is from the memory of the appointed. Memory is therefore for becoming and for willing to become. We must recall what we have willed to do to do it, that is to say, what we have willed to write as a reality (produce and cause to become). Introducing the last step of writing reality:

6. We will it into being from understanding - having willed it into being with, in, and by understanding and therein remembering it having willed to produce it in understanding, by understanding, and through understanding - to write it into being understanding it and understanding that we are presently producing it, causing it into being through the will and in its becoming we understand it is becoming and having become from the becoming we understand it has become and know how it has become from understanding it's becoming process which is a revelation of the work in mind and work from the mind.

We, therefore, have two types of work:

1. Work in mind (which is through sound, in sound, and by sound)
2. Work from the mind (which is in sound, through sound, by sound, and from sound, therefore, revealing sound as its source)

Now, not every work in mind becomes a work from the mind. There are those that remain possibilities in mind as per stage 1 and 2 of the becoming stage; the creation is examined, that is to say, the work is examined in relation to how it can be, should be, before it becomes. We, therefore, find that there is in mind two possibilities of beings and of reality:

1. That which it can be
2. That which it should be

Beings become as they should be to become according to the image and likeness of that which has produced them. Beings are, have become, to begin to become as the Being of beings, the being that produced them. And this that they have become, to become being an actualized possibly from the aforementioned possibilities. But since God is an eternal being and as a being is: so are their possibilities, we find that there are eternal possibilities in God and therein eternal possibilities as to how humanity could have been (possibility 1) but only one possibility of what humanity should have been (possibility 2). Only one possibility of what we should be because what we are is that possibility!

Now the stages of the becoming process are with a process within them. Numbers 1, 2, and 3 are the Thinking Process which is the formulation of Thoughts (ideas which are abstract) which are once again taken through the Thinking Process (number 4) by being compared to the produced Thoughts of the first Thinking Process, what is called the refinement of Thought that results to Refined Thoughts and or Retained Thoughts that are produced through work from mind and it is through these process of thinking in eternity past that creation became and was, and is.

The Order of the Becoming Process

(Order of moments in Eternity Past)

1. Intellect thinks about

2. Imagination conceives in a form that which intellect has reasoned and is reasoning about

3. Understanding conceives what it has imagined and thought of for imagination and intellect are faculties that work correspondingly and to understand we must understand that we are understanding and or seeking to understand and to imagine we must understand that we are imagining; therefore, grasping the idea and the form in the idea

4. Examining through understanding in understanding whether the conceived and the development of the conceived are in agreement and also whether the conceived is according to the design intended from the conception of it in thought and imagination

5. Agree in understanding with the understanding that it is fitting and worth willing therein to say worth producing. That is to say, worth writing as a reality in which case if it is, it is appointed in mind, from the mind, through the mind, and by the mind, and therefore consequently,

produced by the mind for that very mind that has produced it; for we produce a reality agreeable to our minds for our minds which is conclusively a reality that is in our image and likeness

6. We will it into being from understanding - having willed it into being with, in, and by understanding and therein remembering it having willed to produce it in understanding, by understanding, and through understanding - to write it into being understanding it and understanding that we are presently producing it, causing it into being through the will and in its becoming we understand it is becoming and having become from the becoming we understand it has become and know how it has become from understanding it's becoming process which is a revelation of the work in mind and work from mind with both in Genesis 1 being through sound and breath; for it is a living being with breath that spoke it from Himself having thought of it in Himself using the same breath in Him and the sound in Him which is of Himself and Himself.

Chapter 12

TITHES & OFFERINGS' RECONSTITUTING POWER

"Bring all the tithes into the storehouse, that there may be food in My house, and try Me now in this," Says the Lord of hosts, "If I will not open for you the windows of heaven and pour out for you such blessing that there will not be room enough to receive it." Malachi 3:10 NKJV

The first instance we see of tithing is when Abraham tithed to Melchizedek by giving him a 10th of what he had plundered from war. This was before the dispensation of the law. Jacob also promises to give 10th of what God blesses him with to Him (Genesis 28:22). Tithing, as witnessed, precedes the dispensation of the law and was instituted to spring from one's produce in the dispensation of the law. But when Abraham and Jacob gave they gave from their freewill. It was given as a freewill offering to God. Now, joining the dispensation of the law and of ignorance we behold a principle: one can tithe out of anything and not just out of their produce in the sense of salary, in modern times, and or in the sense of the produce of the land alone but one can also tithe from what they make from the sell of their produce of the land having tithed from the produce of the land. There is no limit to what one can tithe from. It is from these two dispensations that we get a clear view and understanding of tithing which is attached to a promise in scripture, from our verses chapter that states God will open the floodgates of heaven and pour out a blessing upon us that we cannot contain when the tithe and offering are brought in to the house of God so that there can be food in God's house. This food in God's house is in reference to the ministry of tithe and offering to the ministers over the house, over the dimensions of the house, and those serving in the house to maintain and keep it. In essence tithe and offerings (freewill offering, first fruit offering, thanksgiving offering) are used to manage the house of the Lord. That is: are used to construct through their management the reality of the house of God (the physical dimension of the house) by meeting the need of the various types of ministers, the poor, the widow, the sick, and the orphans, and stranger in the house of God (those that come about with genuine needs as they pass by the house). Now, the Lord provided for man in Eden by constructing what was needed to meet the needs of man. In truth: needs are met by a constructed reality, as witnessed and seen in Genesis 1. It is from the constructed reality of God that men construct their realities. The materials for meeting man's needs are and were divinely provided at the beginning and in the beginning. It is from these constructed realities by God that humanity meets its needs and, as it relates to tithe and offerings, meets the needs of the house of the Lord. In these meetings the needs of the aforementioned beneficiaries of tithe and offering, there are realities that are constructed in their lives that would not otherwise be constructed. For example, lack of food is a reality, the presence of food is a reality. For some school is not a possible reality, but a reality that is made possible through tithes and offerings. The church changes the latter to the former through tithe and offerings. We see then, that tithe and offerings are constructive agents. They construct the house of the Lord, not only the building but the men in the building that are the house of God within the building known as the Church. Since from what men give they aid in the construction of realities in the lives of others, there is a construction of realities in their lives both physically and spiritually. Spiritually and physically because the ministers of the church, according to their various types, are enabled to serve in the house by having their physical needs met which are essential to their ministering for it is cited: man shall not live by bread alone. That man shall not live by bread alone is to mean that man shall not live without bread. His physical dimension has needs that are met through the physical: the body needs bread. Their ministry to the church is spiritual, they feed the flock with the word of God, that is spiritual. This spiritual ministry to the flock is through the spiritual but the meeting of the church in a physical building is through tithes and offerings. The church is constructed through the aforementioned and as a result, we find that the tithe and offering not only aid in meeting physical needs but in meeting spiritual needs as well. Church construction takes money and needs money. The church is for the construction of spiritual realities in men, and since these men are used to construct the church's physical construction which is used to construct spiritual realities, there is a construction of spiritual realities in men through tithing and offering. Tithing and offerings are constructive and deconstructive agents. They are used to actualize spiritual and physical realities in men as it is written: "I (God) will pour out a blessing upon you that you cannot contain." These blessings are spiritual and physical and not just physical. And every blessing is an actualized reality in man's soul, spirit, and body. We, therefore, see that tithing and giving ones offering constructs ordained realities and are instruments of accessing, so to speak, realities that are blessed physically and spiritually which involve and are connected to the state of the soul. One cannot be used to construct the spiritual and physical reality of God's house and not have their soul's reality and physical reality deconstructed and constructed to the image and likeness of God. This means that tithe and offering has a two-fold effect that is di-dimensional:

1. In the giver
2. In the beneficiaries in the house of the Lord

In truth: tithes and offerings are for spiritual and physical constructions and deconstructions in the Church, building and men. In the soul's construction, the soul is reconfigured, and the realities within the soul, from as far as it's ancestral root (tribe and clan). For the reconstitution of the soul involves its human origin from which it has been constructed. Tithes and offerings are, therefore, deliverance agents. They are used to deliver from ancestral connections and ties for to be blessed with the realities promised in Malachi 3:10, the hindrances to the actualization of the blessed realities and the possible realities therein must be removed, of which ancestral spirits are part of due to the claims they make and have on people through the works of the ancestors (vows, promises, offerings, and sacrifices). Tithe and offerings construct soul realities through the blessed work of the Holy Spirit. For the pouring down of blessings involves the changing of the soul's state which is converting the soul's reality to reverberate Eternity, as appointed at the beginning which is the intended blessed state of God. In truth: tithes and offerings are for the construction of realities in man, his life, and through man having been preceded by the construction of realities in man. Every principle in the Kingdom of God is for the construction of the realities of God and His Kingdom in man and through man so that they can be a harmonic convergence between man and man, man and God and the kingdom of men and the kingdom of God. It is so that: "...Your (God's) will be done (be constructed in men and) on earth as it is in (constructed) heaven."

Chapter 13

PRAYER

"I will pray with the spirit, and I will also pray with understanding." 1 Corinthians 14:15 NKJV

All prayer is in language, from language, by language, and through language which is a faculty of the soul indivisible with understanding. Now, when humanity prays, they pray in either of two languages which are for the construction of the realities of God in them, and through them. In other words, prayer is for the deconstruction of the soul and for the construction of the realities appointed for the soul in the soul. The soul that prayers is reconfigured to configure earth to itself and to Divinity. In truth: the reification process of realities and their examination is to be done in prayer and through prayer. For there is a way that seems right to man and its end is death and men should acknowledge God in all of their ways and He will make their paths straight. And; be anxious about nothing but in everything with prayer and supplication. As it is written: "You will be done on earth as it is in heaven. That is: Your ordained realities be constructed on earth as it is in heaven and in the same pattern they are constructed with. Needless to say, this construction of divine realities and their probable realities therein involves the reconstitution of the soul through the Spirit of God in man through prayer. For this reason, it is written: he that speaks in tongues edifies himself up (1 Corinthians 14:4). To edify means to build, and construct, and in this instance to build and construct themselves so as to reverberate God which involves a deconstruction of the soul and the possibilities inherent in the soul. Whenever there is deconstruction in the soul, the realities probable in that reality that is deconstructed are deconstructed with it. There is no change of soul without a change of the realities in the soul whether in prayer through tongues and or through understanding. It is all for the same reason and works the same work through the Spirit of God (a work of deconstruction and construction). Since we are asked to always be in prayer: the construction of the soul is intended to be ongoing. This means that there are realities generated in us in prayer whenever we are praying and consistency in prayer results in consistency in the generation of realities and deconstruction of realities and their probabilities. The realities constructed through prayer generate probabilities that are to be actualized in prayer through the aid of the Spirit of God. It is not by power nor by might but by the Spirit of God. The phrase: edifies himself means generates realities appointed for himself through the Spirit of God in the language of the Spirit. This is because all construction of realities is through language, in language, from language, and by language. The soul's very reality is sound which is with language: for the soul is the sound of the spirit of man and the spirit the breath of the sound of man.

The change that occurs in the soul affects the spirit of man and any change in the spirit of man affects the soul of man. The spirit is regenerated at the second birth renewing and reconstituting the soul. But the soul must always be reconstituted to construct divine possibilities that are generated in itself through the regeneration of the spirit of man. Regeneration generates possibilities in man appointed for construction. It is the same case with fasting. When man (generic) is fasting, there is a deconstruction of their soul and construction of their spirit. The soul is deconstructed from the image and likeness of the first Adam to the image and likeness of the second Adam whereas the spirit is constructed and deconstructed as well. Constructed to divine reverberation and deconstructed from defilement that is a hindrance to divine reverberation.

The praying man reconfigures the soul. In truth: prayer is, significantly, for this reason (amongst others of cause). Many men used by God have constructed realities for nations that were appointed and constructed the soul's if men through prayer and in prayer. From Daniel to Jesus and such. We see in Paul, Apollos, and Peter the constructive work is God through them in the souls of men through the word and surely and truly enough not besides prayer or in the absence of prayer as evident in Ephesians 1:17 -19; where Paul prayers for the deconstruction and construction of the souls of the

Ephesians. It is through prayer, and in prayer that the soul and its realities are deconstructed and constructed to reflect Infinity. This means that the soul's faculties are transformed in prayer and renewed in prayer. Man's understanding is enhanced as it relates to its capacity to access dimensions of understanding that wouldn't otherwise be accessed. This requires the working of the creation frequency and creation energy within and in the creation frequency. There is an operating of the Spirit of God in man that is a recreating work, so to speak. Even as you read this, and as I write this, there is a working of the Holy Spirit's creation frequency and creation energy in us to enhance the function of our mental faculties and their function as per the will of God for the reverberation of Infinity. For every faculty of the mind was appointed to reverberate God in function. Indeed, if man is to comprehend the Infinite, the faculties of the soul must be reconfigured to will to understand, remember, see (and have Infinity projected in the imagination), desire Eternity, and develop sincere affection for Him. And these, not through humanity but through the work of God in man Who works in humanity so that they can will to act and understand Infinity. Every faculty must be reconfigured and configured to reverberate Infinity so as to have the capacity to contain divine realities and the possibilities therein for construction and actualization. Without reconfiguration and deconstruction, the potency of the mind is limited in its reverberation of Eternity and the development of divine propensities will be lacking because as the soul becomes so it inclines and so it does and as it does so it does from the propensities of what it has become. We find that prayer changes the propensities of the soul in the reconfiguring of the soul. There is no soul reconfiguration and construction without the alteration of the propensities of the soul.

Chapter 14

REALITIES IN GOD

"In the beginning God created the heavens and the earth."

Genesis 1:1 NKJV

God is Eternal. He is Eternity and as such there are infinite expressions of God and infinite possibilities in God. There are infinite possibilities He can actualize. The Alpha dimension of God, from which these realities are actualized in mind and from the mind, is multidimensional. In essence, every dimensional expression of God is multidimensional and has infinite expressions. It is from the Alpha dimension of God that we get variety. In essence, variety is a reverberation of Infinity. God, expressed Himself in variety. We have 7 billion people on the earth and billions of angels, none of which are the same but distinct from another. In so much as there is a homogeneity in femininity and masculinity and the expressions of God in the feminine and the masculine in the make and female, there is, and are, expressions of God in every person as per their uniqueness as it relates to personality, vision, and frequency (every person exists in their own frequency with the creation frequency that is an expression of the Alpha dimension of God and are expressions of the creation frequency and creation energy). Now, the creation energy of God is expressed in the task of creation and in the various types and kinds of creation within

77

the types of creations and the kinds of kinds of creation within the kinds of creations within the types of creations. Every creation exists in its own frequency and energy which are the infinite expressions of the Infinite God, the One Who lives forever and is Eternal. We, therefore, comprehend that there are infinite expressions of the Alpha dimension of God, the dimension from which and in which and from which creation became and exists being sustained by the same dimension and the working of the creation energy within the dimension which, as with the dimension, is multidimensional and with infinite expressions. Every dimension of God is with infinite expressions. There are, therefore, creations we've not yet seen within the types that are present and the kinds within the types and the kinds within kinds in the types of creations. Earth does not carry the fullness of the expression of God. In truth: no created realm, spiritual and physical, has the fullness of the expression of God. It is for this reason that the realities in God will ever be studied on God and in fellowship with God Whose expression in relationship with man and angels is multidimensional in an infinite way. An Eternal being has eternal expressions.

Man, who has been appointed to be used to construct divine realities and to have them within through the Holy Spirit and in the person of the Holy Spirit, Whom man is in and Who is in man, cannot contain the fullness of the expressions of God and the realities in the expressions. The expressions of beings are realities in being and of beings. The divine realities contained in man in the person of the Holy Spirit, increase as man's capacity increases in fellowship with the Spirit of God, Who deconstructs and constructs the realities in man by soul reconfiguration and construction. With every dimension man enters in God, there are realities appointed for construction as per the levels within the dimension. Every dimension and level has a capacity that is developed as per the levels within the dimensions in God for the depositing is divine realities in man and the working of the Spirit in man through the capacity He develops in the man in prayer, listening to the word, and reading of the word. Unless the man abides in Christ through the Holy Spirit and in the Holy Spirit that is one with Him and is God the man cannot be used to do construct divine realities:

"Abide in Me, and I in you. As the branch cannot bear fruit of itself, unless it abides in the vine, neither can you, unless you abide in Me." John 15:4 NKJV

The branch that bears fruit. That is, the man, generic- as used hitherto, has their soul reconstructed and constructed to develop a greater capacity to carry and write divine realities. He is used to comprehend, communicate, and construct divine realities in the lives of others and construct and deconstruct the soul of others via the Spirit of God, and in the Spirit of God that works in the man and through the man. For the Glory of God and the expression of God through the man and in the man.

"I am the true vine, and My Father is the vinedresser. Every branch in Me that does not bear fruit He takes away; and every branch that bears fruit He prunes, that it may bear more fruit. John 15:1-2 NKJV

"If you abide in Me, and My words abide in you, you will ask what you desire, and it shall be done for you. By this My Father is glorified, that you bear much fruit; so you will be My disciples." John 15:7-8 NKJV

These realities that are entrusted to the man via the Holy Spirit and in the Holy Spirit for construction and actualization through the man by the name of Jesus and in the name of Jesus via the person of the Holy Spirit and on the Holy Spirit are of people, places, institutions, churches, nations, families, and schools and relate to the social, economic, and other dimensions of man's life as far as the reality of the body and its condition as witnessed in Jesus' ministry when He reconstructed the body of a blind man, of lepers, and so on by performing creative miracles which are an expression of the Alpha dimension of God and the creation frequency and the creation energy therein. The Spiritual man that is abiding in Christ and abides in Christ from Whom and in Whom man is connected to the Eternal Reality and the realities inherent in Eternity - and Whose Spirit resides and ministers under His leading and guidance - is entrusted with multi-realities with dimensional and realmic ramifications. The realities in God are, therefore, too vast for counting. He is Eternal and they are likewise infinite.

Chapter 15

THE GESTALT OF THE SOUL
(What God Reconstitutes)

"For out of the abundance of the heart his mouth speaks."

Luke 6:45 NKJV

Spiritual realities are the state and condition of the human soul and spirit as per the construction and deconstruction that has occurred and taken place in it through their Adamic origin, tribal origin, clan origin, and family within the clan from the tribe that is connected to Adam; and what has been watched, and heard (listened to), and agreed to. In truth, the soul's constitution is with the aforementioned that form it's the gestalt. It is these that are reconstituted and reconfigured, as the soul is purified for children are reverberations of their parents from Adam, the first of their tribe, the first of their clan, and the first of their family and the family from which they are born. This is what is the macrocosm reality of the soul that determines the possible realities in the soul and the reality of the soul, that is largely, it's spiritual reality. This is through the sanctifying work of the blood of Jesus that disconnects us from the lineage of Adam and the preceding order aforementioned, spiritual speaking, and its effects on our souls to renew and refresh it to the image and likeness of God and to get rid, through the Spirit, in the Spirit, by the Spirit, from the Spirit and for the Glory of God Who is Spirit,

82

of ancestral realities that subjugate our soul's originality and the realities inherent therein. The propensities of our souls are redeemed from the aforementioned ancestral spiritual and soul affinities that limit the function of the soul's faculties as per the covenants and inherited traits that are not in the image and likeness of God. Generational curses and family patterns that are recurring (causing the family to be in a loop) are broken through soul reconstitution and a shift of reverberation from ancestral to divine. These family curses extend to tastes stored in the soul, which form the person's spiritual reality and generate realities being generated in man. The taste of alcohol, drugs, and so forth become constitutes of the soul awaiting manifestation in the generations preceding from the generation that constructed the taste and developed it as part of its reality, inherently and extrinsically. This is the reason certain habits and traits are common in certain families, with the extension generating sexual realities and immoral acts from the person due to the foundation from which they have been constructed. It is imperative to remember the rock from which we are hewn (Isaiah 51:1) in order for us to reconfigure the soul and reconstruct the realities in the soul and the realities from the soul and the probabilities therein, respectively and collectively. Not that all generational traits are reconstituted, rather the traits that reverberate sin are taken out from the soul through the sanctifying work of the blood of Jesus and the Spirit of God.

That is the washing of the Word and the washing of the Spirit and or by the Spirit. The soul is made clean. The realities that give way to demons, and gave way to demons, and have given way to demons, and may give way to demons in the future into one's soul and the realities therein for essokinesis, are taken out of the soul: from the names that are attached to a presence and, therefore, give way to the presence and imparts traits from the presence and the reality of the presence to the person and the presence or presences that operated or operate in the person, to words spoken over the person - words spoken over construct the soul, to names given to the person are dealt with (names speak over the soul, declare a reality in it through the meaning of it, which the soul constructs in actuality), to developed propensities through the media (music, music videos, and movies - Ecclesiastes 1:8), and associative propensities (from one's council, friends, and the company they keep - Psalm 1, 1 Corinthians 15:33). Femininity and masculinity, which are expressions of God in His creation - not that He is female rather that the male and female have an expression of the Infinite; for both are in the image and likeness of God and are part of the microcosmic reality of the soul and were affected at the fall and are affected by the ancestral origin as per the mentioned order in this chapter and in like manner determine the realities constructed by the male and female. We, therefore, find that the expressions of masculinity and femininity is affected by one's ancestral origin and needs reconstitution and configuration to Eternity in order for its expressions, respectively, to reverberate Infinity and retain the originality of the soul. It is the corruption of the microcosmic realities of the soul that has resulted in homosexuality. The aforementioned are the microcosmic constituents of the macrocosmic reality of the soul. It is from these that the soul is made new. The soul is deconstructed and constructed from its microcosmic realities and macrocosmic reality through the deconstruction and construction of the former. Our microcosmic reality affects the realities we actualize from the probable realities contained in our mind.

Chapter 16

VALUE SYSTEM

"For where your treasure is, there your heart will be also."

Mathew 6:21NKJV

A treasure is something of value, and as seen above, where one's treasure is, that is where or what one values above else; and is where their heart is. We need to know that there is a means to value; a manner through which one thing is valued above one thing and is, therefore, preferable amongst other things. This manner of value is a system that affects one's destiny because; value determines priority and we act according to what we value. It is this system that is a guide, a true north, as it were, to all human endeavors. It determines what realities we actualize and which ones we don't actualize. A value system is also part of the microcosmic reality of the soul.

Now, what is valuable is loved, and from this love, it is guarded. The question, however, is: is it loved because it has valued or is it valued because it is loved? Does value precede love or does love precede value? It is imperative to note that if we love something, we will value it. But does it follow that everything loved is valued? And does its value come from the love we have for it? Or does it have value prior to loving it? If its value is by virtue of our love, then it has no value till

86

it is loved. But that it exists means that it has value; if it was otherwise it would have no value because what does not exist has no value. To therefore exist is to have value and not to exist is to have no value. We, however, tend to value what we need over what we do not need but that we do not need it does not mean it does not have value. The value that it has to us based on our needs reveals that we have different types of value systems, that is to say: not everything valued is valued the same way or in the same manner by men regardless of its own inherent and intrinsic value (by existence, and, therefore, by nature - existence is with nature and there is nothing that exists that is without nature). Take the story of Delilah and Samson. Delilah betrayed Samson because he was not valuable to her as much as money was. Samson had value, by virtue of being and by virtue of calling. He was valuable to the nation of Israel as a judge. Both values, that of being, that of calling (which made him valuable to the nation of Israel) were not from man but from God who created him and called him. This introduces us to two types of values attached to humanity (of being and destiny), both of which add to the total value of man. Now, if a man (generic), for instance, was not sane they still have a value in them by virtue of being: he exists and is, therefore, valuable; for all men are created in the image and likeness of God, whether sane or insane. But if, and when, men are not in their destiny, they are not valuable in one way. Men who are, therefore, not in their destiny and or are not in their destiny's dimension are less valuable- by virtue of not being where they are supposed to be. This less-ness of value is in the sense of usefulness because destiny makes one useful in the society, and nation, and therein in the physical realm. Destiny is in fact, usefulness to the society, nation, the church, and nations, through and in one's dimension of calling. The same man who is insane has been made less valuable in the sense that he has been rendered useless by insanity and has no value system; which has nothing to do with being in the image and likeness of God, which makes man valuable not only to God but to humanity as a whole. His value is that of being. But that he is as he should not be, he is not valuable as much to men but is valuable to God. God is the cause of his being. To men, he is viewed with little or no value because he is not useful due to insanity. Though he is not useful in terms of fellowship, and or communication nor in society; he is valuable because he is. Every person that exists is valuable besides their usefulness. Men that know the dimension of their destiny and are not in it, are less useful and in some way, rob value from themselves; for part of their value is in their usefulness. The mad man is also robbed of some value by insanity and as a result is not prioritized by men, not all, but most; for he is rendered unproductive. Productivity is the end of usefulness. What is useful produces.

God's and Man's Value

There is not one man that is not valuable to God. The wicked are loved in their wickedness but their wickedness is hated. Does not God cause rain to fall on the righteous and the unrighteous? God values man. Man's value is from Him. And every man is useful to God: The wicked for the demonstration of God's wrath and mercy and the righteous for the demonstration of God's love and grace. Man has been called to reverberate God in function in their dimension of destiny - where one is set, and or appointed. We become to reflect God in being but and function. Destiny is a function of man as per the image and likeness of God in man. But since it is being that determines function, we find that not functioning in God's image and likeness is not being in the image and likeness of God; that is, not being in one's dimension of destiny is due to the corruption of the image and likeness of God in the sense of reverberating His being which prerequisites goodness of state that results to the goodness of function and in function; which is a common thing in the unredeemed and a struggle with the image and likeness of God and the fallen nature which is common in the redeemed as noted by Paul who stated that which I want to do, I do not do, but that which I do not want to do I do (Romans 7:15-20). The do is a function of being and the want to do and not doing is wanting to function in the image and likeness of God but not being able to due to the sinful and depraved nature of which he, being redeemed was being redeemed from (Romans 12:2). King Saul was useful in function being in the image and likeness of God but did not remain in that stead, and became otherwise; the reason he was rejected and another was chosen, David. Now, King Saul was still valuable to God by virtue of existence but not by virtue of function. He ceased to be useful and therein rejected his destiny wherein was the functioning according to the likeness and image of God, which as previously noted; was a struggle with the sinful nature in the sense of fear which bred impatience resulting in disobedience. Even in our sinfulness, losslessness and lostness; we are valuable to God by virtue of being; and even when men reject their destiny, God still holds them valuable and would not want them to be doomed to hell. Such are punished for their sin here and suffer the consequences.

How the Sinful nature robs and robbed men of value

Man's value is intrinsic and with it, we find functioning value, which is usefulness. The intrinsic gives birth to the extrinsic (usefulness). We, therefore, find that what is without is measured against what is within and or with the within to produce total value. Man's value is the sum total of the extrinsic, and intrinsic (the latter preceding the former and the former proceeding from the latter).

When man fell, Genesis 3; humanity was corrupt, Jeremiah 17:9-10, and the image and likeness of God was corrupt and humanity was no longer good in state and as a consequence, not good in function. Adam remained, had existence but was not as he was to be, that is to say, was not as intended (original intent). Men's (generic) value system and judgement were corrupt resulting to pride, selfishness, deformity, sexual immorality, Witchcraft and so forth as such things as are sins which are too many to mention but not too many not to refer to as done above. Man, therefore, not being in the image and likeness of God due to sin, was now in the image and likeness of sin - not an act that goes against God but nature from which such acts proceed, which is termed in scripture as flesh, and not to mean body but to mean sinful nature from whence sin an act against God proceeds. Flesh gives birth to flesh (John 3:6), to mean that what man birthed was now not in the image and likeness of God but in the image and likeness of sin which was introduced to this realm by man through deception from Satan. Lucifer, being it's originator in the spiritual realm, and, therefore, the father of sin and having birthed it and being conformed to it; all that are of it and in it belong to him and are therein ruled by him being the father of sin. Men were, prior to the sacrifice at Eden, and there to follow till Christ, subject to him and under his rule. Sacrifices prior to Christ being a means of grace to restore man whose sins were covered by that sacrifice which was perfected at the cross with Jesus and in Jesus Who redeemed those who died under the law through and in His sacrifice of grace which perfected and fulfilled the law, i.e, met it's standards perfectly as opposed to the sacrifices of lambs which were imperfect but perfect for the appointed time and were perfected in the appointed time by that of His blood that redeemed the saints of the Old Testament and the New testament.

Now, the corruption of the image and likeness of God meant man was anything other than human, as intended by God. He retained human form which would have been entirely lost had it not been for the sacrifice at Eden and so forth till Christ; and with its lostness that of intrinsic value and likewise extrinsic but being that after sin man remained, we find that before God, there was existing value which rendered men redeemable, able to be restored back to original state and as such original value system. Conclusively: the inherent state of being determines value but being that everything with a state is, exists, it has existing value which is not to be confused with state in men which is intrinsic in this instance. But since whatever is has form, shape and appearance, we find that we also have an extrinsic state, which is appearance or form. Now, the intrinsic state often determines the extrinsic, and as such, we find that deformities without tell of deformities within. Physical deformities testify of inherent deformities. Physical states tell of intrinsic states. This is, however, not always the case, not all men are deformed physically and as such not all physical states tell of what is intrinsic. But when men are gloomy, sad, or hurt, the face will often tell and so will the body when it loses weight and such as are the effects. In some cases, men have even become sick due to deformed intrinsic states. Sickness itself is as a result of intrinsic deformity. By intrinsic I mean, that of the soul and not of the body. Sickness is a testament of man's intrinsic corruption but that they are able to get sick being alive, a testament of man's existing value which is used to restore men back to original intent.

Being that they are corrupt and existing, men are to be valued because they have value even if they are not according to original intent. We are valued by God by virtue of being. Now, corruption requires fixing and human corruption can be fixed. What is corrupt is and that it is, it has value by virtue of being and can be restored to original intent and the value system therein. If it were to be corrupt and not be, it has no value and can, therefore, not be redeemed. Corruption robs value but doesn't destroy value but if not fixed or dealt with; corruption will destroy value with, and in time (the aim of corruption is to destroy value). Being still corrupt and being, there is a value system but not as was or is meant and, therefore, not original and being that the original is lost, a less-ness of value system is present. What is, therefore, a consequence of loss is a tool for use rendering men in their fallen state, potentially useful in relation to original intent with or without man being in original intent; that is to say, redeemed: Genesis 50:22. The potential usefulness being for redemptions sake which is accepted or otherwise by man (seeing that he has freewill upon which God works revealing man to man and humanity's need for God which can be accepted or not after the revelation which has worked a work prior to salvation to result to salvation).

Corruption of state does not render man useless: the useful potential in them remains, though the capacity is affected. Men can, therefore, meet the potential of their destiny and therein fulfil their destiny without being redeemed but miss purpose which is the bigger picture. Now, "can" is not always the case for there are many that die without even knowing their destiny, and others without even fulfilling it having known it, making their death premature deaths. A premature death, in the context of destiny, is dying before one's allocated time (and before fulfilling one's destiny). In relation to the topic, death without being redeemed is corruption fulfilling its end: destruction. Destiny is not the bigger picture but a pointer to the bigger picture which is purpose (God). In the context of making decisions, it is but in the context of life, it is not. To live for destiny is to live wrongly; to live for purpose is to live rightly. Men were created for purpose rather than for destiny.

As to how men generally value things and each other

Men tend to value things based on, as previously seen; usefulness. If something is useful compared to another: it is highly valued; the same applies to persons. If a person is more useful to a man than another, the man will value the useful more. By useful we mean one that is of service to another in some respect and therefore meets a need. There are different ways in which one can be said to be useful, a man of good character can be useful to a man of bad character in terms of confidence when in hardship or for counsel, a rich man is useful though he is bad due to his wealth which is a resource, and is therefore by virtue of his wealth a friend of many (Proverbs 14:20). If the same man was to be of noble character, he'd be more useful to men but would need to know who is useful in his own estate and life. For rich men, whether good or bad, crave a man who is good and can be trusted with his wealth and is, therefore, useful to him by that virtue. Men with wealth will esteem such a man above a rich man who is like them, and yet will esteem the bad fellow above the good one when it comes to enjoying the wealth. It would be good to enjoy wealth with a good man than with a bad one but we see that the bad man is useful in enjoying wealth which is not a bad thing depending on how it is being enjoyed, making a bad man useful in a good way: for enjoyment is good. Now, because money is good, we find that it can be used in a bad way and or in a good way depending on the type of man that owns it. A rich and good man will prioritize wealth as a resource but not before good men or even bad men but will not waste money on bad men, and will, therefore, not prioritize money above the bad man if the bad man will waste it and if not, he will prioritize the bad man above money which is a good thing. A bad man will prioritize money above a bad man and often times above a good man being that money is a priority to him above persons and is, therefore, a priority since it is meeting his need and even if the good man is one that he trusts with his wealth, he will not value him above it seeing that he values him by virtue of his wealth, that he will not steal it but add to it in dealing with it; and not by virtue of anything else. This is usually the trend in business where bad men seek out good men to work for them and are, therefore, priorities due to usefulness in relation to wealth. We, therefore, find that whatever is able to meet one's needs, a man or not will be highly valued, and, therefore, be prioritized above what is unable to. Delilah valued money above Samson. Probably because there was a need he could not meet that money could; hence the betrayal. Priority, therefore, springs from need. Men prioritize what meets need above what does not. This results in relationships where one is useful to another and therefore needed and such so being held more dear than another who is less useful and or not at all depending on the need: of pleasure, money, food, and so on as it depends on need. In most cases when the need is met and the man (generic) is satisfied, priorities will change and the affections likewise with it. But if the affections of need, being from need, have resulted in a knowing of the object of affection, the relationship will not end but remain; if the person in question has been found to be good and is therefore useful as a person rather than as a means, therefore making the imperfect perfect. The imperfect is made perfect because to value by need is to value imperfectly because one is seeking something on account of which there is affection. Once the need is met, affection ceases rendering it imperfect. But seeing one can end up with true affections, based on the person rather than on what they can do for them, which is to objectify, as was the case with Delilah; due to this, we find that the imperfect can result to the perfect once the person is known and is found to be good character-wise. In which case, the man will be valued greatly because they are good and as such of good value rather than of useful value. The latter being perfect and the former being imperfect. But since what is good is useful and what is useful is good; we find that the goodness of usefulness is based on need rather than on being, person, whereas that usefulness from which goodness of being is first prioritized is based on a person rather than on being, therefore, being more perfect. An evil man can even be useful in meeting a need and therefore good for that need but not good in person. No one wants to befriend a bad man though useful to meet a need and therefore good in respect to a need. But everyone wants to befriend a good man and not merely for their usefulness but for their person. It is wrong to befriend a man for their usefulness rather than for their person but at the same time if a bad person will promote virtue in an instance, in that instance it is good to befriend them. Not in another but in that instance where virtue is the final product inherent in which the good man will not have to compromise his virtue and therefore be in that instance bad.

The beautiful, the good, and value

But that something is good does not mean it is beautiful though that which is beautiful can be good. A Lion is beautiful and in that respect good in beauty but not good in the sense that it is a danger to man. We value the Lion for its beauty and goodness as it relates to its beauty but not for its goodness as it relates to our wellbeing (in the sense of the danger it poses). In like manner, there are people that are beautiful and good in respect to their beauty but not good with respect to our wellbeing. Delilah was beautiful and, therefore, good in beauty but not good as it relates to Samson's wellbeing. We, therefore, find that men prioritize what promotes their wellbeing and value it even though it is only good for their wellbeing but not beautiful. In such cases: that which is good for wellbeing is intrinsically good and has an intrinsic effect on the person. But since we are speaking of persons, it also has an extrinsic effect and is, therefore, extrinsically good for the person. And such is the value system of man. This would mean that Delilah was not intrinsically good but was extrinsically beautiful and good in relation to her beauty. She had no virtue, was not morally sound or upright, this is what is intrinsic goodness and, therefore, intrinsic beauty for virtue is that which is beautiful inherently. Samson, therefore, held the extrinsic to be of greater value than the intrinsic; and there are many men who do the same in matters of the heart and also in matters of things. They buy what looks beautiful and as such is good by virtue of its beauty but not by virtue of wellbeing. The consequence to Samson was a loss of vision which meant a possible loss of destiny.

But not all things promote wellbeing in the same way. Medicine for instance promotes wellbeing in health. Whereas something such as a desk promotes wellbeing in finances in the sense that the longer it is able to last, the more money I will save from not having to purchase another that is not long-lasting. In that respect, it is good for my financial wellbeing. In purchase, men value what is good for their financial wellbeing and as such in using money they look at what is worth the money, that is to say, measure its value with its durability. They, however, not only purchase what is good for durability but also what is beautiful. A man would at any chance go for what is beautiful and durable and not only what is durable. Men would go as far as letting the durable pass to look for the beautiful and durable and most likely to pay more for that which is both as opposed to that which is either or. In most cases, however, they overlook durability being blinded by beauty. That something is beautiful doesn't make it durable, and likewise to the durable. It can be durable but not beautiful and it can be beautiful but not durable but a durable thing can be beautiful and a beautiful thing can be beautiful. Therefore, not all beautiful things are durable and not all durable things are beautiful. If the durable and the beautiful are side by side along with the beautiful and durable at a sale; men are most prone to value in cost the beautiful then the durable but prior to both the beautiful and the durable. It is financial wisdom to purchase the durable and the beautiful, and or the durable in last resort if the beautiful and durable is absent than to purchase the beautiful and not durable which is a loss because one would have to purchase another when the beautiful get ruined and they are fools who go for the same rather than learn from their error. It is also likewise expensive to repair it. The cost in a total fix might well be enough for a new one of the same type or another of a different type.

We, therefore, find that men value the beautiful, the durable, and the beautiful and the durable; with the order depending on one's value system. Now, men are loves of beauty and that is why they so easily settle for the beautiful over the durable. They all love the pleasure which the beautiful provides. That which is beautiful is pleasurable to behold and for the pleasure of seeing they choose the beautiful over the durable forgetting that the pleasure of seeing is transient. Everything that is beautiful without will eventually fade. This is the case even in men and women relationships (with durability referring to virtue in men and women). Men and women are so easily driven to the beautiful rather than to the durable and or the durable and beautiful.

Adam and Eve were driven to the beautiful and therein choose beauty over the beautiful and the durable, the tree of life. We, therefore, find that to be content with beauty is to be foolish in choice.

Why men value the beautiful

The beautiful is chosen in the assumption that it is without as it is within; an assumptive measurement of beauty and its goodness with durability, and its beauty. The beauty of durability is wellbeing and that of sight is beholding. The former without durability becomes contemptible and the latter without beauty seems less valuable but with beauty more valuable. Another reason why men chose the beautiful is due to them being lovers of beauty. Every man is a work of art having been created, and therein is a work of art, and are likewise drawn to a work of art.

Beauty journeys to beauty:
Kin to kin; type to type;
And likewise kind to its own.

All men are lovers of pleasure: for art, of which they are a work of, is a source of pleasure. They seek out what they are but not at all all that they are. For some being beautiful without, and not within, seek beauty within and without; and this for the reason that all men, even in their corruption, long for that which was originally theirs. For original intent is such that beauty and durability are one whereas corruption separates the two. Nature determines one's value system. We value as we are and choose as we value. This does not mean that if we value the beautiful above the durable we are beautiful. On the contrary, it means that we have a liking for the pleasurable rather than durable and this a working of the sinful nature that divides durability and beauty using the latter to blind and causing durability, which has been split from beauty, to be despised as much due to the same amount of blindness being used to blind from beauty and if at all, even with more effort due to the promotion of wellbeing. Beauty was, therefore, intended for wellbeing as much as durability was. The two are the same sides of the same coin and to split the two, as did sin, causes a split, a corruption, of wellbeing, and in wellbeing.

Wellbeing the means through which to value

Now, it is then wise to conclude that wellbeing is the end of which we aim but not the end we get due to the split of beauty and durability on account of sin. We must, therefore, value by wellbeing rather than beauty only. For as we have seen the beautiful on its own does not cause wellbeing and neither does the durable but both when joined. But even when not joined: the durable is to be valued above the beautiful and the beautiful and durable above the durable and the beautiful. The durable and beautiful are more valuable than the beautiful. But there are in men degrees of beauty. One is fairer than another and so on; and so we find that durability is to be looked for prior to beauty for one greater in beauty is not always greater in virtue (durability), and is, therefore, not good for one's wellbeing. It is advisable for the single in pursuit of marriage to marry the beautiful and virtuous. For beauty on its own without durability is empty of wellbeing and beauty with durability for one is not durability for another. Men have different durable needs based on their own person and good: good for one is not always good for another. Each one has a need and needs the beautiful with its compatible durability, that is one that the man and or woman needs for their wellbeing. Compatibility of beauty is not at all compatibility of virtue and hence no wellbeing will be produced. There must be compatibility of durability (of virtue as well as of beauty); the result of which is a posterity that is far fair in beauty and far fair in durability for:

> Beauty journeys to beauty:
> Kin to kin, type to type;
> Every kind to its own -
> For preservation's sake.

The Beautiful and Durable Separated

As previously noted the beautiful is not necessarily durable and vice versa; and this is as a result of sin, as proved. I aim here to further what I've set forth in the previous chapter.

Beauty is that which is pleasant to look at and behold and is, therefore, sensual and a work of art is thus visible (which qualifies it as sensual); for sensual means to be able to be experienced by the senses. Now, to be perceivable means to be visible and to be visible means that something exists and if it exists it must be caused and therein have an origin (a cause); for it is an absurd thought that something can cause itself; which means it would have to be and not be at the same time, an impossibility. We, therefore, find that beauty is produced, caused to be and if so a work of being for it is a being that is able to produce which tells of intelligence. Tells of intelligence because beauty is a work that is produced and being produced, it is through a process and therein an intelligence and or an intelligent being; who is also beautiful, for as previously established kin births kin.

To say that something is beautiful would be to mean that it is pleasant to look at (Genesis 3:); which would deem a process of reasoning had taken place to therefore result in the statement; it is beautiful. Beauty then is a cognitive experience of that which is without. Cognitive experience because to see and not understand is not to know what is seen and therein have no appreciation for it. It takes reasoning to know beauty which is an examination. The object in question is examined holistically; looked at as a whole and not at all in parts. Looked at as a whole because everything has parts which make it up and the parts are with their own fairness that contribute to the fairness of it as a whole. The whole, therefore, is how the parts relate to each other; whether they are agreeable or not and or compatible in form. Form because the eye only sees the form. If there is no agreeability of the whole, there is no beauty. But we must have in mind, before making it a rule of third; that parts relate differently and therefore complement each other in different ways and therefore are beautiful in different ways; being that this beauty is that that men consider beautiful by examination with preference of person having some influence. So, we find that to one man a certain agreement is beautiful and to another, another one is not. Oftentimes or not; what one man considers beautiful is not at all what another does. But both men can agree on what is beautiful besides their taste. We, therefore, find that there is what is universally beautiful and what is preferentially beautiful. There is a form that is universally fair and agreed upon to be fair by all men based on its agreeability with its different parts. This being that all parts are somewhat proportional, that is to say, possess sameness of size and, therefore, agree in size. Size because to have form is not to be without size; whatever has form has size. Beauty is, therefore, by form and size. Both being inseparable; conclusively summing beauty to be about agreeability of size in form and or of form and the size of its parts to each other, what is called symmetry.

But since form and size have shape, we find that shape matters as much and if anything it seems to matter much. Shape has to do with boundaries of the parts, and size is of course a contour that brings out shape therein defining form; that is to say, producing shape. We, therefore, find that shape is produced by the definition of form irrespective of form. Irrespective of form for it is form that is shaped and every form is shapeable to some particular respect. To some respect because there is a limit to shaping form, least we shape it to its demise which would be disintegration. A form is therefore beautiful based on the size that contours the shape; to set size is to shape. Shape is, therefore, dependent on size and is somewhat, based on this, a synonym of size in the sense that it is a product of it and is not without it; and often in referring to one or the other the one or the other not referred to directly is referred to indirectly. The size here being as it relates to every part of the body and how it relates to every other part. Having stated that men have different tastes, we find that some prefer a symmetry of their own, by their own I mean as it relates to their own taste whereas still, there is something that all men can agree to be beautiful introspective of their own taste and also respective of their own taste (this latter one being in the sense that men can and do oftentimes or not share tastes and can therefore agree to something being fair on account of their agreement in taste). We, therefore, find, having stated that size contours form giving it shape, that these contours are what make something appear beautiful and or seem beautiful therein being beautiful. This beauty being of form, that is to say, body.

Clothing and beauty

Men and women, in their respective clothing, have about them (the clothing), a form that is brought about and seeing that clothes are for men (generic); we find that clothes are made according to form, that is according to the contours of a body (we shall examine this later). The reason they are clothes of all men and women according to their respective shapes and sizes; and these clothing bring out and or do not bring out the beauty of the man or woman. In bringing out the beauty of a man and or of a woman, the clothing must, as previously stated agree with their contours. But the clothing in and of itself must have its own beauty to bring out the beauty of the one wearing it. By bringing out beauty we do not mean revealing nakedness rather decency. Since the charm of beauty is decency (a thing to look at later on). Back to clothing, beauty reveals beauty and as such it must be beautiful to be said to bring out a person's beauty of which, this beauty must be in the sense that: (a) it fits the man or woman, (b) it must agree with itself, it must also have symmetry being that it is made in mimic of the male and or female body, (c) the color and all such attires must be according to the preference of the person. On point c: men prefer clothing in colors due to their own skin tone and or to what color agrees best with another type of color that they want to wear the other color with, what is often called color blocking. We, therefore, perceive that in the purchase of clothing men prioritize one color above another based on their preference as it relates to their skin tone and or in relation to what they'd want to wear it with and therefore will perceive it as a need. Indeed, even in shopping for clothes we are acting from a point of need, for clothing is a need, but the need for clothing is distinct as it relates to preference as this far seen.

Seeing, as we have above, that men have their own skin tones and such and are of varied colors, so to speak- not offensively intended, we find that even in what one considers to be beautiful there is a preference based on skin tone amongst men. Some preferring one particular over another and others preferring another over that and or two of different types from among many other types and these that they prefer they value above other types based on what they consider to be beautiful as it relates to form, for color is part of form but not form in seeing that we have different colors of people, we have different preferences besides contours to contours with skin tone or color. As such men will prioritize a beautiful person who is of their preference in matters of skin tone, and contours above one who is of their preference in matters of contours but not skin tone. Priorities, in the sense of marriage but in the sense of friendship of which if it is the case, it is then termed as racism which is a sin belonging to the class of murder since to hate a man or woman is to have killed them in your heart (1 John). Men will, therefore. prefer to settle down with what they consider beautiful color wise and form-wise and in that respect value according to that particular need of theirs in terms of marriage; for their preference became a need. Preference is in fact an expression of need, for men seek out what they prefer rather than what they do not.

They are, however, men (generic), with a preference of contour but not of color and as such will prefer a particular contour regardless of color and in this respect value the contour alone and therefore seek it out as a need for marriage. Not that either of the above or the aforementioned is better than the other in some respect, except in the sense of racism, but that each is good in respect to the needs of the person. We therefore conclusively perceive that men consider something to be beautiful according to their own preference and prioritize it so, that is to say, according to their preference, and therein it finds value from preference and is of value.

Now, clothing despite any preference is of value to man but having that men have different preferences, clothing is valued differently, according to preference and, therefore, valued differently. But all in all, the general value of clothing is in the covering of beauty. For that is the end of a cloth; to cover beauty. For the beauty of the body is not at all for every eye, as to every man there is a wife and every wife a husband, beauty must be covered since it is not meant to be revealed to all men. The honour of beauty is in covering and the glory thereof in its revealing. Beauty should be honored and that which covers it must likewise be honorable and since honour produces decency, and in fact, honour is considered to be a trait of decency, decency of dressing is honorable and the former not at all honorable.

But there are clothing that are for different occasions and in that respect, each is a need as per the occasion but even on the occasion, there is a decency to be maintained. We, therefore, find that value of clothing, and its beauty is as it relates to an occasion. If I am going swimming, I have no passion for a suit, and it is not a need as per the occasion; and if I am going for a wedding, I have don't have a need for a swimsuit; it is not an occasion for a swimsuit. The right attire for the right occasion is not, however, decency, though it is part of it; part of it because to have worn as the occasion demands is to have decency in part; what will make the decency complete and, therefore, decent, is whether there is modesty as it relates to the appropriate covering of beauty.

What then is appropriate or modest dressing?

Modest dressing is as it has been noted; one that fits the occasion and covers beauty. For to cover beauty is to honour oneself as physical beauty belongs to the person rather than the person to the beauty, which would be idolatry; in which case the covering will be minimal or not at all- there would be inappropriate dressing. In which case seduction is prioritized and valued above the modest when beauty is an idol.

Modesty and decency in dressing are such that there is a covering of the body in a way that the male and female organs are covered appropriately. Where the aim is seduction and sex besides the confines of marriage, there is no modesty. The breasts of the female and their sexual organ when covered appropriately is modest. Even when in the swimming pool, these two in cover are a show of modesty. The aim in the pool should be to cover and not to reveal, when it is to reveal, there is seduction. It seems that modesty is contingent on the occasion and, therefore, the type of cloth will be prioritized and valued as per the occasion and modesty. If valued besides modesty, there is no decency. But we must ask ourselves whether the body is covered appropriately means revealing the shape is descent. Is it enough to cover the breasts and the sexual organs only? Should the body be covered entirely and is that what is appropriate?

I have stated that the clothes must agree with the shape but not in such a way as to seduce, as is the common trend of today's time. This not only applies to women but to men as well. Hugging clothes are not appropriate rather they are seductive. Shape and size is God given but shape and size should be covered honorably and appropriately as the temple of the Holy Spirit. This applies to swimming pool as well. I hold that the body should be covered in such a way that the glory is honored and covered to avoid seduction.

Culture and the beautiful

Everyone is born into a culture and is therefore in some respect from a culture, and as Mahatma Gandhi said; people are their culture. Being that they are so we find that people are formed by their culture and therefore end up perceiving beauty differently as it relates to culture. But seeing that we have different cultures as per the continent, the nation, and the home; we find that there is a complexity in every perception of beauty in everyone. We, therefore, have different types of cultures which determine beauty:

Continental culture

Each continent had a similarity of culture in one way or another. People of Africa share some beliefs and some cultural perspectives based on that continent's perception of things. Which is what is called a worldview.

Africans, North Americans, and generally look at beauty as a means and portrait of their tradition. If it reflects the African culture of tradition, it is beautiful. It is tradition that Africa is known for, and as such whatever is able to reflect tradition is beautiful, and will therefore be prioritized and valued as such because there is a value of tradition, and we, therefore, find that there is a conservativeness of some sort in the perception of beauty from a continental perspective since the aim is the preservation of tradition. One that prioritizes tradition will be viewed beautiful above one who does not as tradition is a people's beauty, in the sense that that is their way of life. As such, one who is preservative in and by nature will be valued as beautiful over one who is not even when her beauty is by preference. Men, therefore, look for preservation of taste by having that which they have a taste for.

National culture

Each person has their own nationality, and in their nationality, there is a perception of what beauty is; which is dependent on that nation's culture.
House or home

In every nation, there is a home. The home is intact the foundation of a nation. It is the building block upon which a nation is built. Nurture takes place in the home where manners are taught and therefore forging perception of the beautiful based on what one has been taught by their parents.

Tribal culture

Different tribes have different cultures. The Jews, the English, the Americans, the Agikuyu, and so forth as per the many tribes in the many nations and therein is a desire to preserve the tribe which would make one desire to settle for their own tribe based on certain stereotypical perspectives of different tribes. As such beauty will be viewed from a tribal viewpoint and prioritized as such and therefore have value above another tribe seeing that the ones of the same tribe are kinsmen and men will often value their own above what is not their own.

The above are some good, but the problem with them is that they fail in some way to perceive the beauty of humanity. For they are in my own view, mists to a true perception of beauty. True perception of beauty is recognizing humanity above the aforementioned. If anything, they should aid us to form a perception that appreciates and celebrates diversity rather than one that appreciates and celebrates one sort or type of humanity. After all, we are all made in the image and likeness of God in regards to the aforementioned. Not to mean there is no beauty in them, rather that there is a tendency to lean towards the extreme resulting in deaths and even more to loss of humanity. They should, as previously stated, aid in the perception of the beauty of humanity which is appropriately and right seen through the eyes of God (Genesis 1:26-27).

The 4 cultures determine in some respect the dressing and, therefore, with its modesty. With most African nations being conservative and most countries of other nations being likewise conservative and others not based on that of others and or of that of what is agreeable in terms of humanity as modest. Different cultures have different views of modesty, and so forth but we find that true modesty is to be rightly viewed through the person of the Holy Spirit and His leading, as it is stated; He will lead you into all truth (John 14:6).

The beauty of things besides men

We've already mentioned clothes as being beautiful based on preference and modesty and or lack of it, therefore. We also find men will generally seek out the beautiful first being that they are a work of art themselves and therefore want a beautiful house, car and so forth, and therein prioritize it having valued it. But seeing that things are of different brands, men will have an inclination towards what they consider a brand that brings out beauty perfectly as opposed to another. They will prioritize a brand that is beautiful above another and, therefore, value it more and be willing to part with whatever the sum of it is or less of what it was after a bargain. Men automatically prioritize and value beauty perceptively.

Durability

Durability is a virtue (and refers to virtue), as previously stated and these being intrinsic as opposed to extrinsic and seeing that sin separated virtue and beauty; men are less likely to notice virtue at a go. They are more prone to notice beauty at a go than durability, which is an inherent beauty. The extrinsic is always easily notable. But as previously noted; the beautiful is not always good for a person, though it is good for beauty; and though beauty is good, beauty is not at all equivalent good for wellbeing. We, therefore, find that durability needs time to be perceived. And what needs time to be perceived is perceived through examination. And that is a common factor between the beautiful and the durable, the difference being that the later needs more time whereas the former needs little time.

Durability and clothing

It is not enough that something is modest. It must be durable and therein promote wellbeing, financially that is. If it is not at all durable it is a loss rather than a gain and a loss is not at all good for wellbeing. Many men have fallen sick due to loss and loss has led to the end of marriages and so forth.

If an article of clothing is durable and modest it is of greater value than s cloth that is modest but not durable and if it is durable and not beautiful but modest, it will be of more value compared to the beautiful. But men will often value the former over the latter due to the need of being seen as beautiful and or of beauty. The need of being seen as beautiful has to do with the agreeability of cloth with one's contours. In such cases, men will look at the material, because in terms of clothing, shoes, and even utensils, and beds, cars, houses, and furniture, it is the material that determines the durability, not appearance. But that it looks beautiful and is durable, it will be more valued than one that is beautiful only and not durable and likewise to one that is durable and not beautiful.

Culture and durability

Based on the different cultures, we perceive that durability is also as such and from what preservation of culture is one thing deemed durable and or preferred over another. That one is of the culture of the continent, nation, tribe, or fits one's home culture and is therefore beautiful culturally speaking makes them culturally durable. Introducing types of cultural durability:

- Continental
- National
- Tribal
- Home

But that one possesses one or two, or all of the types of durability does not mean that they are inherently virtuous. Cultural virtue is not a personal virtue. Men will therefore value either of the two dependently or together depending on what between the two they value most and or if they value both the most. This means that they are men that will value cultural virtue above personal and those that will value personal above cultural. Of which between the two, the latter is wiser than the former because one does not marry their culture but the person. One does not live with culture but the person. Culture shapes the person, as previously noted but culture is not the person but is part of the person, and the wellbeing of culture is not the wellbeing of a person. Yet again, there are those that will value cultural and personal virtue and look for it wherein there is the wellbeing of culture and the wellbeing of a person. This split is a consequence of sin. Cultural virtue is not at all meant to be split from personal virtue but to fuel personal virtue and make it better. It is therefore wise to value personal virtue above cultural virtue. This means that we don't have to be from the same culture to be good for each other, but we can also be from the same culture and be good for each other.

In cases where the durability of culture and or a people is prioritized above the durability of humanity, resulting in xenophobia; an evil. Bringing us to the durability of the nation. Where we find that all men are naturally patriotic and or tribesmen, being of that nation and from that nation, they generally want the best for that nation and its people and being of that tribe desiring the best of that tribe being from that tribe and of that tribe. But where we find xenophobia is the result; we find that we are not at all being humane. It is worth noting that we are humans first before we are tribesmen or of a nation. We find this truth amplified in

God's word where we had humanity before we had tribes and or nations. God created humans first before creating the tribes and nations from which we find that tribes and nations are preceded by humanity. Tribalism is therefore a sin. Durability of tribe, and nation, is good but it is not good when it is at the expense of humanity. What it means to be human is being in the image and likeness of God and not being of a certain tribe and or from a certain nation. Equality is not based on tribe; it is based on humanity. To therefore be tribal and or xenophobic is not at all to be human. The durability of tribe and nation above humanity is not a virtue but virtue defiled.

The value of nations and tribes is inherent in humanity. It is virtuous to value humanity above tribe and nationality but it is also virtue to value tribe and nation but when it is at the expense of humanity it is not virtuous but virtue defiled. This is so because tribes and nations were and are in a human rather than a human being in a tribe and or a nation. If we are to truly be humane, xenophobia and tribalism would not be an issue. As with the others, the split of humanity, tribe, and nation, is a result of sin. Sin splits, and in itself is a split. There are, therefore, men (generic) who value tribe above the nation, and therefore value tribe above humanity and those that value nation above tribe and therefore value humanity, and there are those that value humanity but do not value tribe and nation and, therefore, do not value humanity at all and there are those who value tribe, nation, and humanity all at once rather than one or two of them with humanity being the chief value. To indeed value humanity perfectly, is to value tribe, nation, and humanity. For humanity is the source of tribe and nation. Valuing proceeds above precede is evil and results in folly and more evils with it. The precede thereto being God. For tribes, nations, and humanity are from God. We, therefore, find that to fail to value God who is the precede of all results in xenophobia, tribalism, and inhumanity.

Sin split the beautiful and the durable causing wrong and wicked value systems that are not at all for the wellbeing of man. This split is what God did not intend and as such thereof not being original intent. Beauty without virtue is a consequence of sin and beauty with virtue a consequence of original intent. To, therefore, be restored to wellbeing, we must be restored back to God from Whom sin split us from. Corrupting the image and likeness of God and the reverberation of God that can only be restored through being born again (John 3:3,3:6). It is, therefore, impossible to have a proper value system where there is a split of man and God but possible to have such a system where man and God are in fellowship as is the cause of Christ's coming. Making the second coming of Christ also a means of restoring beauty to virtue (durability); and beauty to virtue in man and in the dealings of man.

To conclude the matter: a sound and humane value system is found only in God, and therein stating conclusively, as per this stand of the chapter - and retrospectively from the chapters' prior- that destiny requires God as the center of the person meaning: purpose is greater than destiny and, as such, men ought to live for purpose rather than for destiny. It is only through a Christ-centric life, that one can actualize the best possible realities.

Chapter 17

ESSOKINESIS

"...in which you once walked according to the course of this world, according to the prince of the power of the air, the spirit who now works in the sons of disobedience, among whom also we all once conducted ourselves in the lusts of our flesh, fulfilling the desires of the flesh and of the mind, and were by nature children of wrath, just as the others."

Ephesians 2:1-3 NKJV

Reality is constructed in mind and is from the mind. It is constructed in mind through a becoming process that involves deconstruction and construction with evaluation and finally agreeing to actual construction from mental constructions that are in the mind. That is, from a variety of probable realities in mind. Now, there are things that have been constructed in time past and time present and those to be constructed from time to come. While they were not, there is how reality was and when they became there is how reality became. Reality was one way before them and another after them! This means that reality is malleable, it can be changed and what is authored is what changes it. What becomes changes what is, with what is becoming being the secondary reality, man's produced and created reality, from a probable number of realities that exist in the mind that are generated by humanity as per their soul's microcosmic realities and macrocosmic reality, and what is being the reality constructed by God, what is the primary reality. It is from the latter that the former becomes because man is what is part of that primary reality, which is constructed by God. Man was constructed to construct in his image and likeness as God constructed in His image and likeness. Man was created in the image and likeness of God to construct in the image and likeness of God therein bringing glory to God. This is what worship is; constructing from that image and likeness of God (as in the beginning).

What is Essokinesis?

Essokinesis is the ability to manipulate reality, that is to say, the ability to change what is to be something other than what is and or seem what it is not causing it to suit the reality desired by the one with the ability.

God is the Alpha reality, the reality from which all things created by Him proceed. Now, that means that God has the ability to manipulate reality. He can change whatever is to whatever He desires. In creation, He constructed reality to that which He desired, to His image and likeness when it came to man and to good as He is good when it came to the rest of creation to reflect His goodness and glory. All that God made was and is matter, it was constructed from matter which He constructed, meaning that He has the ability to manipulate matter in the atomic and subatomic dimensions; the latter being quantum kinesis and the former being atokinesis.

Man is a reality and he constructs a reality (secondary reality). He constructs it as he has become and as is becoming and in that particular sense he has the ability to manipulate reality because he alters the form of what is to cause what is not to become from it. He constructs a building from stones by manipulating the form of the stone. It remains a stone but it takes a different form other than the one it was in before. The very act of deconstruction and construction of reality in mind, by the mind, through the mind, and from the mind is essokinesis to some degree. But being that reality is constructed from the mind and in mind, and by it and through it, the one that is truly practicing essokinesis is the one that is manipulating the mind. This manipulation of mind being the manipulation of the thinking process of the individual.

When man fell, the enemy had access to him, and he could, therefore, manipulate the thinking process of man and therein manipulate the reality of man. He now had essokinesis and could practice it in man while in man through demonic oppression and possession, and through thought projection which does not necessarily require the former mentions. By virtue of the fall, the two happen and also by the same virtue man had given him access over his realm and he could, therefore, determine the reality man was to write and wrote in this realm (the secondary reality). He became a contributor to its writing:

"And you He made alive, who were dead in trespasses and sins, in which you once walked according to the course of this world, according to the prince of the power of the air, the spirit who now works in the sons of disobedience, among whom also we all once conducted ourselves in the lusts of our flesh, fulfilling the desires of the flesh and of the mind, and were by nature children of wrath, just as the others." Ephesians 2:1-3 NKJV

- The prince of the power of the air - Satan
- The spirit - the person that is Satan
- Who now works in the sons of disobedience - to mean in their understanding by manipulating it and their thoughts through the thinking process. These sons being those that are not saved (though those that are saved can be manipulated when they are living in sin by thought projection and or possession
- Fulfilling the desires of the flesh - operating in the desires and understanding of that image and likeness of the enemy

He works to get man to construct a reality that reflects him in every respect. He had done this in Sodom and Gomorrah, and at the time of the destruction of the earth in Genesis 6, creation had been conformed to the image and likeness of the second lot of fallen angels which agree with the enemy hence their thoughts were consistently wicked and corrupt:

"Then the Lord saw that the wickedness of man was great in the earth and that every intent of the thoughts of his heart was only evil continually." Genesis 6:5 NKJV

- The wickedness of man become great - man consistently authored a reality contrary to God's image and likeness
- Every intent of the thoughts of his hearts - every reality he intended to author from his thoughts which were preceded by a thinking process which was according to the dimension and level of wickedness he had reached and the level inherent therein
- Was only evil continually - was ever becoming as he was becoming for we think as we have become to think and imagine as we have become form what we have become.

Man as Malleable

Man changes, we are one way at one time and another way at another time. We are becoming beings. Spirit, soul and body. All of the dimensions of man become. He grows in spirit, soul, and body with all those dimensions and their becoming is man's becoming, which was to ever be towards God. There are, therefore, 3 dimensions of becoming in man with two of them being metaphysical because they involve that which is not material. Now, that means that that which is living in man becomes. What makes him a living being which we have established to be soul and spirit, becomes.

In the beginning, man was good and after the fall he became corrupt. Genesis 1:31, and after Genesis 3, he became evil and corrupt, Jeremiah 17:9-10. From good to corrupt is a testament of his malleable nature that is further attested to in Romans 12:2 and 1 Corinthians. Being that men (generic) are malleable, every dimension of their lives is likewise so and reflects what it is they have become; for they construct their dimensions as they have become. This means that every aspect of our lives reveals what we have become, what we are, and they morph as we morph. Our soul reality morphs as we morph. Our physical realm morphs as we morph. It is our morphing that morphs our physical reality. As we grow in understanding, we morph, and what we do, the reality we construct, morphs. With the fall of man, Satan was given authority over the becoming process of man and could manipulate it to his advantage. We see examples in scripture where the enemy manipulated a person's reality and their becoming process:

- Samson gave the enemy access to him through sex and the enemy manipulated his reality via Delilah causing loss of vision
- Solomon through sexual immorality via his forefather Judah. Same applies to David
- Using the spirit of fear to cause neurokinesis, thought manipulation, and therefore essokinesis for we construct reality from thoughts and in thoughts: "For God has not given us a spirit of fear, but of power and of love and of a sound mind." 2 Timothy 1:7 NKJV

Having access to Adam and Eve meant that the enemy had access to the seeds in the man, and the seeds in the woman and could manipulate them causing infertility in both and the seeds in both while and in conception. He could, therefore, manipulate and manipulates the three dimensions of man in the becoming process in the womb and from the womb:

- Spiritual
- Soulish
- Physical

The spiritual he could affect through the soul (but does not have access to it rather defiles it by defiling the soul), and the body through the soul and or by itself as with the soul by itself. With the former being echokinesis (manipulation of sound resulting in dumbness, autism, deafness, and so forth) and the latter atokinesis (manipulation of atoms and therein the manipulation of matter even at the quantum level) which results in deformities and lack of proper development, miscarriages and so forth. With these came the manipulation of the integral fusion of the body, spirit, and soul; the three-stranded cord:

"...a threefold cord is not quickly broken." Ecclesiastes 4:12 NKJV

This means that he has access to the becoming process in the womb, and from the womb through having it in the womb. Ancestral spirits, which are evil spirits, given access to a person and their generations, affect the becoming process of the child while in the womb and also from the womb. Demon oppression begins in the womb and as a child grows they grow with that spirit oppressing them and manipulating their reality as it integrates itself to their becoming process which it also manipulates.

Now, there are two ways through which the enemy manipulates our reality: a) from within, and b) from without. The former is a means to get to the latter. He manipulated the thoughts of Eve from without and when she bought the lie, he could manipulate the reality of man from within. The manipulation is often dimensional, that is to say, focused and centered in one dimension of our life. With David, Solomon, and Samson the manipulation was in their relationship dimension. It is different with each person as per the ancestors' choices and or as per our own choices. There is not one dimension in our lives that the enemy cannot manipulate if we give him the right and access. Indeed, he seeks one to manipulate by scouting and seeking access. He tried it with Job, but there was a hedge (a covering of protection) in all of his dimensions as revealed by Satan's statement to God:

"Have You not made a hedge around him, around his household, and around all that he has on every side? You have blessed the work of his hands, and his possessions have increased in the land." Job 1:10 NKJV

We must keep our coverings intact through the aid of the Holy Spirit so that the enemy does not have access to our reality and the dimensions therein:

"Why have You broken down her hedges, so that all who pass by the way pluck her fruit?" Psalm 80:12 NKJV

"You have broken down all his hedges; You have brought his strongholds to ruin." Psalm 89:40 NKJV

In the beginning, man was hedged, but sin removed and exposed that covering that was over him, exposing himself and the generations in him to the enemy. The devil could not touch him unless man exposed himself by removing the hedges:

"You have hedged me behind and before, and laid Your hand upon me." Psalm 139:5 NKJV

The segmented and integrated nature of Reality

Every personal reality contributes to the reality of the physical realm. The physical reality is the sum total of personal realities. Kings of nations are appointed by men based on their personal reality, that is to say, what they have become which involves their spiritual realities which is a dimensional reality in the metaverse that contributes to the reality of their realm, that is to say, their home and themselves, for men are realms in and of themselves with them being a realm within a realm in the metaverse which they determine. Every man is an authority over their own reality. They determine what to write and what not to, what becomes their soul content and what does not with what that does becoming a determining factor in the construction of their reality in mind and from the mind which becomes the reality of the physical realm which is a realm of manifestation of what is in mind which is according to one's soul content. These personal realities are specific but contribute to the reality of the physical realm. By manipulating personal reality, the enemy manages to manipulate the national realities, and therein the physical realm for if he is indeed to have the rule over the physical realm and author a reality that is in his image and likeness, he must manipulate man's reality because it is men that appoint leaders over nations and determine the reality of their nations which are kinds of realms within the physical realm.

Chapter 18

DIMENSIONS OF ESSOKINESIS

"...in which you once walked according to the course of this world, according to the prince of the power of the air, the spirit who now works in the sons of disobedience, among whom also we all once conducted ourselves in the lusts of our flesh, fulfilling the desires of the flesh and of the mind, and were by nature children of wrath, just as the others."

Ephesians 2:2-3 NKJV

Man is an integrated being with 3 dimensions, soul, spirit, and body, and as seen in the previous chapter, the enemy manipulates the reality of man through having access to the man, and this access was given to him in Adam who was the realm in which all men were. For all men were in Adam and when the enemy had access to Adam, he had access to the seed of Adam in Adam and could manipulate the seed of Adam and the seeds of men from Adam, the seed for life and the seed of life, respectively and collectively. Now, the becoming process begins in the womb and therein, as previously seen does the essokinesis start as per the two dimensions of man, respectively and collectively. Two because the enemy does not have access to the spirit but can access the soul, and the body through the soul and the soul through the body. We, therefore, have two dimensions of essokinesis: soul and body.

1.   Soul essokinesis

"Be careful little eyes what you see...Be careful little ears what you hear...When flattering leads to compromises, the end is always near..." Casting Crowns (Slow Fade Song)

The soul is the sound of the man and is home to the following faculties: imagination, memory, understanding, will, emotions, and desire (inherent in which is taste). When Adam fell, the enemy had access to men and to their soul and could manipulate each of the aforementioned faculties according to his will. The reason it is written: "...the spirit who now works in the sons of disobedience, among whom also we all once conducted ourselves..." Works in the sons of disobedience to mean fallen angels deceived by Satan, men given over to Satan in service, men conceived through and in the power of the enemy, and the unsaved. We see three categories of sons of disobedience, all of whom are under the influence of the enemy but at different and to different degrees. The manipulation of the unsaved is in the soul from whence reality is crafted in mind, and crafted from the mind through the 6 stages of becoming and thence we find that he manipulates the imagination, the understanding, memory, and desires to his likeness and image for the writing of a reality reflective of him. It is this that he did with Eve outside Eve.

he worked without to get within and works the same way till date: from without to get within by appealing to the imagination, the understanding, and desire which are faculties of the soul.

"So when the woman saw that the tree was good for food, that it was pleasant to the eyes, and a tree desirable to make one wise, she took of its fruit and ate. She also gave to her husband with her, and he ate." Genesis 3:6 NKJV

- When the woman saw that the fruit was good for food (desire/appetite) - reasoned about the statement that she was told and formed a perception from that statement made by the enemy through thought in her thinking process that involved her imagination which she perceived through the eye to see that the fruit was good for food, which is to mean that it appealed to an appetite for food which was given by God
- Pleasant to the eye (imagination) - appealed to the imagination which sees through the eye. It is the soul via imagination that sees through the eye
- Desirable to make one wise (understanding) - able to increase understanding and therein give wisdom

Eve remembered what she thought about the fruit, then she took it and she ate it. The statement when she saw; shows a conclusion from her thinking process and a conceived idea in the mind from her thinking process which involves the entire faculties of the soul. We remember what we think, and remember what we have seen and have seen to think about and do in relation to what we have seen and are thinking about. Satan began working without to get within, to begin working from within. Once within he could manipulate the faculties to his own desires. In today's world, he still works from without to get within through what we watch, and what we listen to. Through music and videos - motion images- he captures our understanding, and our imagination therein having access to men through sound and imagination. The latter can generate images in mind and the former can create sounds in the mind. There are times when we hear it to imagine it, and times where we hear it to think about it, and other times where we see it to imagine it. He is able to manipulate our reality by what we see, and what we listen to, which grants him the ability to influence our thinking process and the thoughts we produce which are the realities we write. While within, he creates an appetite and propensities of what gave him access to strengthen his hold on us and establish his manipulation. There is always a descent towards addiction and or towards likeness and or affection towards the things of the enemy without a know. In the development of affinity, there is attachment and we end up feeling as though we cannot do without it.

Other manipulations under this include:

- Academic manipulation - the manipulation of one's understanding making it difficult to learn and process knowledge

- Financial manipulation - access to the soul is access to the dimensions of the life of the soul

- Sex manipulation - premature ejaculations, lust, illicit sex, and lack of satisfaction during sex between husband and wife

- Image manipulation - the projection of visions and dreams that are demonically generated and claimed to be of God. It is from this that we get false visions and dreams

- Relationship manipulation - relationship is a dimension in man and not a dimension outside man. When the soul (imagination, and understanding) is under manipulation so is the relationship dimension (which we will look at in detail in another chapter)

2. Body manipulation

"So Satan went out from the presence of the Lord, and struck Job with painful boils from the sole of his foot to the crown of his head." Job 2:7 NKJV

Every motion of the body is a movement of the soul through the meta-body of the individual. When the soul is manipulated, so is the connection between the soul and the body and the connection between the meta-body and the physical body. This involves the manipulation of the intricate fusion between the body, soul, and spirit. When the integration is manipulated, the body becomes sick and falls ill. There are illnesses that are due to the manipulation of body and soul relationship for when the soul is sick, that is to say, is under demonic oppression, the body is likewise so and the reality of the person becomes perceivable by the spirit in them. There is an animation of the body by the spirits through which they experience the physical realm and perceive the meta-realities of people via the one they are oppressing; through the person's imagination due to having access to the soul of the person via a dimension or via the person's self-giving to the enemy, for those in service to the enemy are given over to him and through them and in them, he experiences the reality of men and sees their meta-reality. Now, the experiences of that soul become shared by the spirit in the person. As he sees so they see, as he tastes so they taste, where he goes so they go. The body becomes a tool for them, and it becomes a portal for them through which they can accomplish their assignments (every demonic assignment has a physical dimension for the aim is physical manifestation). While in the soul, through the integration of their frequency with the person's frequency, and with the body and in the body via the soul, the spirits can use demonic darts to attack the body and introduce sickness (Psalm 9:5) with the aim of killing, destroying and stealing - cutting short one's life (premature death).

Job was attacked by an illness from the enemy in Job 2:7: "So Satan went out from the presence of the Lord, and struck Job with painful boils from the sole of his foot to the crown of his head." His attack on the body of Job was not via the soul though the soul experienced the pain. There are, therefore, two ways through which the enemy attacks the body: a). Via the soul, b). Directly. The first is an attack that is from within and the former is an attack from without which is always centred on the soul, from whence man decides and will from having reasoned about the action and imagined the action. The enemy's attack on Job was on his body to cause him to curse God and sin against God as was the case with Adam and Eve, He attacked from without to get within and attack from within.

Chapter 19

SLEEP MANIPULATION

"And no wonder! For Satan, himself transforms himself into an angel of light. Therefore, it is no great thing if his ministers also transform themselves into ministers of righteousness, whose end will be according to their works." 2 Corinthians 11:14 -15 NKJV

Man has two states: the sleep state and the waking state. In the waking state arrows of lust and so forth can be thrown causing one to lust after another and so forth. In the sleep state, one can be terrorized by evil spirits and frightened by the same through demonic dreams and spiritual activities in the metaphysical universe which are aimed at manipulating the reality of persons and the probable realities therein. It is for this reason that King David wrote:

"You shall not be afraid of the terror by night,

Nor of the arrow that flies by day,

Nor of the pestilence that walks in darkness,

Nor of the destruction that lays waste at noonday." Psalm 91:5-7 NKJV

David was covering his sleep state and wake state, respectively and collectively, from satanic manipulations through pestilence, terror, arrows, and destruction in the various means that the enemy employs them for reality manipulation.

Spiritual Morphing

To morph and or transform, as per the spiritual context and meta context, is to take another form, to shift from one form to another, to take up a form that is not of yourself, to masquerade, and, therefore, not be true but pretentious. Satan and his ministers, angels and men, transform into ministers of righteousness who are of the light, in the literal and not figurative sense, with demons masquerading as angels and men as servants of God serving under the powers of the enemy and in those powers deceiving men by teachings and introducing doctrines contrary to truth. It is these demons, which are principalities, that are behind every false doctrine with each having and producing its own teaching through dreams and or other means to the recipients that are to be used for deception.

"Now the Spirit expressly says that in latter times some will depart from the faith, giving heed to deceiving spirits and doctrines of demons..." 1 Timothy 4:1 NKJV

It is at this juncture that I want to state, as per a previous chapter in this book, Faith: our theology and theological perceptions and understandings determine the reality we author and the probabilities from those realities in mind, and from the mind as per our object of faith. Joseph fled from Potiphar because of his theology. What you do and or do not do, has a strong propensity that is inclined and rooted in your theology. One's theology, which is metaphysical in nature and is about the metaphysical, also opens one up to metaphysical realities in their dream state. It is for this reason that pagan kings such as Nebuchadnezzar had dream interpreters that were not of God. They were astrologers and magicians who had interpreted the dreams of the king in times past. This opened up the dream state of the king to manipulation that extended to his wake state. Whenever men seek dream interpretation through other means besides God, they open their dream state to manipulation and their reality because dreams are projected in the imagination which is a faculty of the soul, from which and in which realities reside and are generated in with their probabilities.

"Therefore I issued a decree to bring in all the wise men of Babylon before me, that they might make known to me the interpretation of the dream. Then the magicians, the astrologers, the Chaldeans, and the soothsayers came in, and I told them the dream; but they did not make known to me its interpretation." Daniel 4:6-7 NKJV

"Then the king gave the command to call the magicians, the astrologers, the sorcerers, and the Chaldeans to tell the king his dreams. So they came and stood before the king. 3 And the king said to them, "I have had a dream, and my spirit is anxious to know the dream." Then the Chaldeans spoke to the king in Aramaic, "O king, live forever! Tell your servants the dream, and we will give the interpretation." Daniel 2:2-4 NKJV

Spiritual Cloning

Spiritual cloning is a spiritual process done by demons where they change form by stealing somebody's image and imitate their frequency through frequency modulation to deceive men and propagate the enemy's agenda. In order for the cloning process to take place, demons must have access to someone's life through sin. There are two major ways the images are used:

- Use of your image and or people's images by demons
- Use of your image to clone someone else in the spirit

Use of your image and or people's images by demons

One of the reasons why demons conduct spiritual cloning is because it is easier for us to trust people we know and are familiar with. Through the images of the familiar, demons manage to get people to agree with them, enter into covenants, and commit sin in the spiritual realm through dreams, which are a reality in the metaverse with metaphysical and physical implications. It is not only with the images of people that we know that the enemy causes us to sin or enter into an agreement with in the spiritual realm; he also uses the image of the people we lust over. By this, the enemy manages to gain access to people and to manipulate their reality. The probable realities inherent in them and the realities to be actualized from the and the probable realities from the actualized realities.

I have dealt with such cases with the most recent being a week ago. A young lady I have been walking with asked to meet me and told me that she had a dream where she slept with a girl that she knows. Upon hearing the dream, I knew (through the Holy Spirit) it was not the girl but a lesbian spirit that had cloned itself using the image of the girl with whom, at one point in time the girl who had the dream had pretended to be lesbians with and approached girls. Though they didn't sleep with any girl, the action of pretending to be lesbians, opened the door for the lesbian spirits in both and for their cloning. Thankfully, God delivered the girl through prayer. If not dealt with her life would have been under manipulation in the most devastating of ways through sexual acts with girls.

Use of your image to clone someone in the spirit
There are people that have been turned into another person's clone in the metaverse. With the ramifications being for the switching of destinies, hatred, and rejection by destiny connectors, potential suitors, and trouble in peoples' lives aimed at the three agendas of the enemy: kill, steal, and destroy. This happens in cases where we are living in sin, are ignorant of the metaphysical nature of life, are a threat to the enemy, are not alert during our sleep and have not sanctified the sleep state to God which is for meta-activities. Not every dream is a dream, there are dreams that are meta-activities in the metaverse. That are realities taking place in the spiritual realm as per our lives.

I had a dream one night where I saw someone throwing a face my way to turn me into a clone of someone else. I was able to tell who the face belonged to. But before the face was integrated to mine completely, I woke up and began to pray against cloning and took off that face in the spiritual realm. I recall the name of the person to whom the face belonged, that the person was a pastor while one earth but seemingly never got to fulfil their destiny. I saw their story as the face was being thrown my way, their struggles, and their state which was to be imparted to me in the dream; the end of which would have been poverty, abortion of destiny, and rejection due to the changing of my identity in the metaverse.

When one is turned into a clone, the enemy gets access to them via the process and they become like the one they have been cloned after, taking their image and likeness in the metaverse which is with a meta-reality that has physical implications. There is, therefore, an impartation in the cloning process which causes people to lose their reality in the metaverse and in the physical. It is through this process that the enemy steals destinies, chances and privileges inherent in destinies causing reality manipulation (essokinesis). We have people experiencing difficulties because they are clones of other people in the metaverse that are either dead or alive and under the enemies control. This drastically changes their reality and the construction of their realities in mind and from the mind.

Chapter 20

RELATIONSHIP MANIPULATION

(Extract from Scribbles Scribbled Thoughts)

"Two are better than one,

Because they have a good reward for their labor."

Ecclesiastes 4:9 NKJV

In dealing with men and relationships, you must comprehend that there is always a preference. As such, you must present an idea of "perfect beauty". Make it so pleasing that they fall in love with the woman or man in their mind (who doesn't exist). Unbeknownst to them, they will compare the real with the unreal and love the inexistence. By this act, you will achieve delayed marriages, and if you play it out well; no marriages at all. They will keep looking for what doesn't exist and if they happen to have a little glimpse of light in the tunnel you have placed them in, by meeting someone who fights the idea, remind them of the "perfect qualities of the one the one woman in their mental construct. Our Foe will often bring several women to get the fellow and fellows to the lady till the imaginary gives way to the real. He will have them face the truth of their existence and of beauty, that there is none that is truly perfect but rather that each is perfect in and with its imperfection. I know! It sounds absurd but it is, believe me, a truth, a paradox! The idea behind our Foe is

149

that in accepting one with their imperfections the little nit wits will have reflected their relationship with Him and with it His nature. This takes us back to the fall when our dear Father corrupted the image of God in them. Our Foe aims at taking them back to Eden. Our aim and that of our Father below is to keep them from Eden and take them away, further away in whatever way possible. So, when one begins to cause the idea of "perfect beauty" to fade, remind them of the qualities they fell for and convince them that the person does exist. Tare them from the reality of beauty, that it is with elements of imperfection (wherein lies the reality of the fall of man). Throw in hope if you have to. As a matter of fact, use it. Cause them to hope for what doesn't exist to keep them from what exists.

In stating that you, my dear students, should make them hope for what does not exist in place of what exists, I mean that you should make them desire what is nonexistence because what they hope for exists. The Foe works in a manner that whatever hope He places in men for things that exist in Him and or have existence already from Him and therefore are. The woman or man that is hoped for is, having already been in the Foe, and having become from the Foe. Knowing this aids us to deceive; deception is most sweet when it is for the inexistence; indeed, false hope is truest when what is hoped for does not exist. The Enemy does not have them hope for what is not; though in their immediate, their present, it does not exist and likewise that which they hope for, in the sense of person, also exists in the same state as they do; in expectation of what is but is not. It is in its own reality but is not in their own reality but both are in the same reality in that they exist in the physical realm, the earth. Our aim is to cause them to hope for what is lacking: "perfect beauty" and, therefore, miss true beauty. You see my dear students, true beauty is perfect imperfectly and therein perfect perfectly but false beauty is perfect perfectly without imperfection, which is unbecoming of humanity while they walk this earth, and this is what we would have them desire.

Allowing them to know the above draws them to Eden, deceiving them and causing them to love perfect beauty that is nonexistence takes them far from Eden. This takes us back to the fall when our dear "Father" corrupted them. He aims at taking them back to Eden. Our aim, and that of our "Father", is to keep them from Eden and take them away, further away in whatever way possible with the end being Hell. Allow me, at this point, to regress to a previous point on hope, well the kind that we are to arouse in them. I stated that we have to make them hope for what does not exist, which is called the hope strategy. By this strategy, they will search and look for what does not exist, and when they think they have found it, by thinking they have found it - I mean when we have brought and caused them to fall in love with a girl or boy of our choice who has perfected the art of pretense- by being one way but yet is not as they seem, who is of cause part and parcel of our kingdom and walks according to our ways, they will find out that they have not, and we ought to repeat this several times to cause them to lose the desire for marriage altogether, and if we cannot we cause them to have delayed marriages. You have to understand that the aforementioned is a perfect tool for causing and creating anachronistic realities in their lives. There are times set for them to walk into marriages, and we seek to have them miss these times and the seasons inherent therein, which is having them exist in our reality, rather than in the reality of what is written about them, which is His plan for them, the aim of which is drawing them to Himself and revealing His love and mercy for them by using marriage itself as a means. Do not be without sense, you must understand that marriage, as it is written in Ephesians 5, is appointed to reflect the nature and relationships of God with them. The institution was created to reverberate the person of God. It was intended that both male and female, who are reverberations of Him in their distinct genders, ought to reflect Him together. The man to see Him in the woman and the woman to see Him in that man through the expressions of the masculine and the feminine, which find their fullest expression in Him, which is of cause, something we have managed, with the media, to avert and we ought to do so consistently and deprive them of this Edenic truth. The fall gave us access to the feminine and masculine to manipulate, and we have done so for centuries. The woman has been looked at as lesser in reverberating Him and the male as His perfect expression. We have managed to deprive her of her role in the Church, Marketplace and confined her to the house where her role is likewise under our hand: her job is to give birth, to take care of the house, and comfort the husband through sex. The other way is by developing a perspective that is "educated": that the woman can do what the man can do and not only do it but do it better. This is the motto of most of the earthly women development and empowerment movements, which is our doing. We had to retaliate when they began to get enlightenment regarding the woman. We gave them a learned and educated view to counter His view, which is Edenic. As a matter of fact, all you pastors, teachers, apostles, prophets, and evangelists, use the scripture to propagate this view. Tell them, using Genesis 1:26-27, and the appointing of the male and female over the earth, that both have authority and that both can do whatever the other can do because both were appointed together. This plants a seed of discord, and disunity in the marriage, the woman will see herself as the head by our ways after the seed is planted, but the man is the head. Confuse the roles to confuse the home.

Hitherto, education has been a good way to manipulate the expressions of the female and male. We use it to counter revelation. An educated woman who sees herself as an equal to the man in role and function, and that she can replace the man in his function is a product of our educational system. It is a most pleasant tool to use, teachers take note of this. In our schools, you are the prophets, the apostles, the pastors, the evangelist, and the teacher. Teach them our word from his word. Emphasis on our doctrines. We have for the past few centuries elevated education above the church. The market place is more hailed than the church. It is more attractive, and even most of the so-called Christians have our view and doctrines built in them. We have managed to cause the wives of pastors, and even the pastors themselves, to hold this doctrine by the challenges we have brought their ways and those He has allowed them to go through for His glory and their good, we have managed to corrupt by planting a seed of doubt in them. It is for this reason, that many women see themselves and consider themselves better than men. They are trying, even those in the church, to be men, though unconsciously. They are extreme feminists, propagating our doctrines to their children and coworkers. Arguing with their men, and are not submissive to them. All these due to education. You see, the educated woman, or by our own doctrine, the truly educated woman, we have managed to develop the mindset that the man is a tool for sexual pleasure and for progeny. She has all she needs and so why need a man? What good is a man when all she has is at her disposal? If she has the desire for children, give her the idea of sperm implants. Let her see the seed of the man more important than the man. As such, marriage will not be a factor nor a reality to be actualized. We aim to propagate this philosophy. Soon, marriage will be a byword. And if the lady desires sexual pleasure and to conceive through it, manage to get her to see it as a tool for progeny, not for anything else. Let her get pregnant and end the relationship. It is in fact better to get her to have one night stands in search of pregnancy than to get her into a relationship with a man, who may want to play a role in the child's life.

Now, when it comes to Christians the above applies but it is categorically important to get the spiritual to marry the carnal. We have managed to ruin many by this working. You see, my dear students, not every believer is the same. They have dimensions and levels in the dimensions with different visions and destinies, which must be compatible for the function of both in their destinies, for the glory of the Lord of the Spirits, and their own good. Which in all truth, we'd not have them known and as such we have made them blind to this truth by teaching that spiritual compatibility is all about being saved, as they usually put it. The carnal becomes a dimensional gateway to the spiritual to frustrate and hinder the walk and effectiveness of the spiritual. The former has propensities of the flesh, lust, greed, anger, hate and so forth; which are ours and attract us. We have a legal right to enter their house, corrupt, and work against their marriage on account of the carnal, who according to their book; is a friend with us and enemy to their Lord (James 4:4). They do not know that we know this much, and it is better that we have them not know. Ignorance, as previously stated, is bliss to us, and harmful to them, but we will have them oblivious of this truth. With the carnal, we can project our thoughts, and images for actualization.

You must grasp that relationship is not a dimension outside man but a dimension in man. They are relationship in themselves, as He is in Himself. Manipulating their relationship dimension is, in essence, manipulating the soul which contains realities that we can manipulate to fit our own desires and eventually, which is the goal, have them author realities that contain probabilities that agree with who and what we are increasing our influence in their lives and world. This was the case with Samson, Solomon, and David. Though we could not destroy them, we managed to attack them and wound them, changing their realities and the probabilities therein. For David and Solomon, it began from their forefather, Judah, who had lustful propensities. We amplified this in Solomon and managed to introduce pagan propensities in his life through our women. See how we began with the ancestor and used him as a gateway to access his generations. Unless they change their ancestral (tribal and clan) propensities, they are food for eating. And when they have separated themselves, they are ancestors in the making and we can begin to find ways into them to access their generations and their realities. It is for this reason that the carnal believers are our friends. Understand that where the marriage foundation is not based on the Lord of all spirits, we have access, where the marriage is in the church but sexual immorality between the two is unconfessed and there is no repentance, we have access; where porn is a norm in their lives, we have access.

We have developed a misconceived idea amongst believers that we do not start fights marriages while they are in a marriage or when they are in a relationship. Not that we don't. The truth is: we begin to fight this long before either by manipulating their becoming process, which begins in the womb. It is from there that we begin fighting marriages because marriage is part of their becoming process. It's easier to destroy a seed than a full-grown tree. From the time they are young, we develop perceptions and views that will favor our agenda and propensities that are in our image and likeness for the authoring of realities that reflect us and agree with us. These give us access to their lives and themselves for manipulation.

Chapter 21

ANGELS

"Are they not all ministering spirits sent forth to minister for those who will inherit salvation?" Hebrews 1:14 NKJV

Angels, like men, have realities to actualize from a varied choice of possible realities as well. They are with will, understanding and such as are the faculties of the soul that are God given! Each and every single one of the angels has their ultimate reality to actualize (destiny to fulfill) as it relates to the reason behind which they have been created by God. Angels were created before men, and watched the creation of the earth and rejoiced together in unity as its foundations were laid and settled by the person of God (Job 38:4-7). It was angels that cast down Satan and his angels. The war was not between God and Satan but between the angels of God and those of Satan with the former being led by Michael. "And war broke out in heaven: Michael and his angels fought with the dragon; and the dragon and his angels fought, but they did not prevail, nor was a place found for them in heaven any longer. So the great dragon was cast out, that serpent of old, called the Devil and Satan, who deceives the whole world; he was cast to the earth, and his angels were cast out with him." Revelation 12:7-9 NKJV

Now, these angels of God, minister in nations and the physical realm, and in the lives of men as per the book of truth that have been written by the person of God, for the fulfillment of the actualization of realities and the possibilities inherent in the realities actualized that reflect and reverberate God, and also to aid men fulfil their respective destinies (actualize their ultimate reality from other actualized realities that result to the aforementioned), and the destiny of nations and therein the destiny of the physical realm as a whole. Their main end and work is to synchronize our realities, and that of the physical realm, to the times and seasons that are contained in our books of truth, which is the mind of God for the nations and the mind of God in the nation. Their concern is the will of God, and they respond to the word and will of God and not to the will of men. We cannot command angels! They respond to the word of God, and carry out His counsel, not the word and counsel of men. They are given assignments as per their destinies and each knows their place and their role and by this we have their ranks and orders which are for the actualization of God possibilities in the physical realm:

- Principalities over nations
- Authorities in nations
- Powers in nations
- Angels given charge of men

The realities angels are called to actualize are integrated to that of men. Their operations are for the purpose of creating a harmonic convergence between the spiritual realm, the Spirit realm, and the physical realm in the word, through the word, and by the word of the Word, by the Spirit, in the Spirit, and from the Spirit, and through the Spirit who works in them and through them. Angels like men become in soul content, though they do not become in body. They learn about God in fellowship with Him Whom they reverberate in their aurae and glory due to the integration with Him and in Him through Whom also, they minister to us and fulfill His will and administer it in our lives by ministering to our souls, spirits, and body. Their ministry as that of men, touches the three dimensions of men involved in the dimensional construction of our realities and the possibilities generated from these realities. The body must be touched, the spirit, and the soul. The Lord has a will for the flesh and ministers to it, as He has from the genesis of creation and the becoming of man. The realities we have been called to actualize are not actualized besides the ministry of angels which is for the same cause.

Chapter 22

THE MEDIA

"The eye is not satisfied with seeing,

Nor the ear filled with hearing." Ecclesiastes 1:8 NKJV

It has been noted in previous books, and most detailed in the Metaphysical Nature of Life, as per the preceding books of this series; that the media is a means of accessing the soul of humanity. We shall now look at this in depth (as is perceived to be sufficient). The eye and the ear are portals to the soul, and not only them but every opening in the body of man is a portal. And as noted the eyes and the ears function in a reverberation of the law of infinity and for this reason the eyes and ears are never satisfied, that is; are never full. The soul which sees and hears through the two is never full. There is always accumulation but never fullness. Such is the capacity of the faculties of the soul. They have limitless potential because they were created to understand the limitless. And as noted in a previous chapter in this book: the faculties have dimensions that they grow in. In truth, every faculty was created to reflect the nature of God. To be a reverberation of Infinity. It is from this understanding that the enemy and his army work from. They comprehend the elementary principles of the being that is man and our constituents. From that understanding there is the exercise of the manipulations of the kingdom of darkness. There is not one place that this is truer than in the media which is used to access the understanding and the other faculties of the soul which are responsible for the crafting of realities in man and from man.

Dynamics of Manipulation through the Media

There are projections of sexual immorality, and thought projection through music and movies that are in the Babylonian frequency and are in with a negative vibration. It is well noted that there are things learned from watching and listening. In truth, music and movies are projections of realities that exist and or realities that are appointed to exist in men through their projection in the media and through the media. About 10 years ago or so, there was a telenovela aired by one of the mainstream media stations in Kenya where the men wore shirts that revealed their chests, half way. It didn't take much time before that became part of the culture in Kenya. Of which I'd become part of. Looking back at it now, it is seen and was seen as an expression of masculinity. This was, however, a manipulation of the masculine and a projection of lust and sexual immorality through lust. Women in the same show wore clothes that revealed their cleavages, and as was with the feminine expression so there was in the women in Kenya, not all of cause but many were taken by it. And as it was with the men, it was with the women. While it was perceived as a fashion trend, it was projections of spirits if lust, and lust propensities, and the corruption of the expression of God in the feminine and masculine. It is the plan of the enemy that the feminine and masculine expressions of God in humanity be converted to his image and likeness and become projections of himself. The language used in the songs propagate the same, and the dancers, and clothing and themes in the song propagate whatever it is that has been appointed for projection through the media to humanity. The media is, therefore, a portal through which the enemy accesses a home and the people in the home. Care should be exercised when it comes to what we watch and what we listen to.

I recall one time when the Spirit of God spoke to me about a gospel song that projected pride. I wondered how that was possible till I examined the lyrics, as per the leading of the Holy Spirit. The song, through Christian, had bars and lyrics which were of the flesh, and in the flesh. The glory was not upward to God but rather to the one that was singing the song through the exaltation of the gift above the gift Giver. Whenever men exalt the gift above the Giver, it is pride rather than worship. It is an act of the flesh rather than of the Spirit. For whatever is of the Spirit glorifies God rather than men. It is God-centric not man-centric. Such are many of so called Christian songs.

Now, it is also important to note that whatever we constantly associate with through the media and in the media, we meditate on. It becomes our meditation and every meditation becomes a soul content that will be actualized. It becomes a reality in man before it becomes a reality from man. As it is written:

"This Book of the Law shall not depart from your mouth, but you shall meditate in it day and night, that you may observe to do according to all that is written in it. For then you will make your way prosperous, and then you will have good success." Joshua 1:8 NKJV

Your favorite song(s) becomes your meditation which in turn becomes part of your soul content and an agent of soul construction and deconstruction through constant meditation via the realities being projected in the song. It is because of the aforementioned principle and working of meditation in humanity that music and movies have been used to introduce perverse language that have become a norm in society. But the goal has not been, and was never the language of men; but the soul of man through the faculties. It is so because language is inseparable from the soul which functions by the same, in the same, and through the same. By perverse language, many have had their reality accessed and manipulated through the universal law of homogeneity (like poles attract in the spiritual realm and unlike poles repel). Perverse language attracts perverse spirits (a working of the law of homogeneity).

www.ingramcontent.com/pod-product-compliance
Lightning Source LLC
Chambersburg PA
CBHW071215240726
48654CB00009B/800